Astrology for

The Ultimate Guid

Zodiac Signs, Numerology and Kundalini Rising

Table of Contents

Introduction

Thank you for purchasing *Astrology for Beginners: The Ultimate Guide to Astrology, Zodiac Signs, Numerology, and Kundalini Rising.* Inside this book, you are going to find all of the information that you have been searching for about yourself for a long time.

You have probably tried to look up some of this information on your own in the past but ended up feeling overwhelmed and unsure about where to go once you found the information you thought you needed. That's okay; the subject matter in this book can be a lot when it is not organized. We are here for you though.

We have compiled information on the following topics for you:

- Astrology and its history
- The Zodiac Signs
- The meanings of the Zodiac
- The Chinese Zodiac
- Birth Charts
- Numerology
- Your personal numbers
- Kundalini
- And so much more!

Consider this the companion that will help you discover who you are, where you came from, and where you were meant to go in life. There was no subject too big in this category that we didn't give you some insight on.

Make sure that you spend some time on the Kundalini section to learn how to awaken the energy that you hold inside of yourself. The power of breathing and meditation as well as exercises to help you obtain the yoga goals that can free your mind and spirit.

It is human nature to want to know who we are and where we are meant to go. It is also even better when we teach you about the potential of your cosmic energy!

So enjoy this journey, and good luck on finding exactly who it is you are meant to be!

Chapter 1: Astrology and Horoscopes

History of Astrology and Horoscopes

When the men, philosophers, and scientists of ancient times looked up to the sky, it was too big for them to fathom. During the day, a large hot sun rules, while at night, a cold moon shines in the distance surrounded by thousands of star groupings. These men couldn't decide about how to learn about them, that is when astronomy and astrology were born.

One group needed to explain the sky scientifically. They formed astronomy, which is the study of the sun, moon, and stars using scientific knowledge. Astrology, however, was formed by those who believed that the sky told so much more than could be scientifically explained. They believed that these objects in the sky were heavenly bodies that had an effect on the aspects of human existence.

You can thank the early Babylonians for being the first civilization to understand that the sky held more than just the sun, moon, and stars. They were the first to use twelve distinct constellations and the planets and track their movement as they passed through the heavens. These twelve segments are linked with particular times of the year. The Babylonians used this to predict weather patterns for planting and harvesting schedules.

The Egyptians took the segments a step further from the original Babylonian configuration. The Dendera Zodiac was split into decans. These decans were separated by ten degrees in the sky. There was a total of thirty-six decans. This is the beginning of the modern calendar system that shows the months and the days. The

The Dendera zodiac - Louvre

Egyptians were also the first to assign elements to their decans.

In the coming centuries, the Greeks jumped on board with the idea of astrology and the twelve segments that the Babylonians originally pointed out. The Greeks are the first to give them the name "Zodiac." These concepts eventually boil over into the Roman empire as well. Using the zodiac became a popular and dramatic thing in society. It was used to tell the fortunes of men and women during the time, giving astrology and exciting reputation.

It was the combination of the Egyptian principles with the Greek/Roman ones that created horoscopic astrology. Horoscopic astrology is what is most commonly practiced today. Horoscopes have become more of a novelty item for most; the seriousness has been lost over the years. Horoscopes are primarily based on the astrologer's interpretation of the sun at the given moment in time they are deciphering. The most common point in time used is the person's day of birth. The alignment of the sun and the planets at that time can tell a lot about a person's life.

The first printed horoscopes in the newspaper were reserved for those people who were famous. Much like the 1916 Boston Sunday Post horoscope of President Woodrow Wilson. Since then, they have done nothing but rise in popularity. There are some skeptics who do not believe that astrology can tell that much about a person's personality, love life, and fortune based on the constellations in which they were born under or the planets in which they were aligned with.

Thirteen Other Types of Horoscopes That Exist

- Alchemist Horoscope
    - This horoscope combines numerology and astrology that are defined by ten different elements from the periodic table.
        - 1. Silver
        - 2. Iron
        - 3. Mercury
        - 4. Zinc
        - 5. Tin
        - 6. Lead
        - 7. Platinum
        - 8. Nickel
        - 9. Gold
        - 0. Copper
    - You calculate this horoscope by taking the individual digits of your birth date and add

them together. The figure you get will have two numbers, so you add those together as well to get one number.

- Arab Horoscope
    - Just like the Western horoscope, there are twelve signs assigned to the horoscope. These signs are named after medieval weapons.
        - Spear
        - Sling
        - Ax
        - Dagger
        - Club
        - Mace
        - Knife
        - Scimitar
        - Machete
        - Chain
        - Poniard
        - Arch
    - Each has a lucky number, which has a lucky weapon that is correspondent to the place they were born.
- Aztec Horoscope

- Animals, objects, and plants are associated with specific symbols and twelve signs. The signs aren't associated with a period of birth, but rather the particular day.
    - Deer
    - Caiman
    - House
    - Flower
    - Snake
    - Jaguar
    - Reed
    - Rabbit
    - Eagle
    - Monkey
    - Flint
    - Silex
    - Dog

- Celtic Horoscope
  - This horoscope has the most signs underneath it. They are all named for trees.
    - Olive
    - Oak
    - Birch
    - Beech

    - Fir
    - Poplar
    - Maple
    - Hazel
    - Hornbeam
    - Chestnut
    - Cedar
    - Cypress
    - Ash
    - Fig
    - Apple
    - Walnut
    - Elm
    - Pine
    - Willow
    - Rowan
    - Linden
- Chinese Horoscope
  - Consists of twelve animals and is broken down by birth years on a cycle of twelve years.
    - Rat
    - Ox
    - Tiger

        - Rabbit
        - Dragon
        - Snake
        - Horse
        - Goat
        - Monkey
        - Rooster
        - Dog
        - Pig

- Druid Horoscope
    - Druids were the great magicians of the Gallic period who had the responsibility of watching over the divine. They praised nature, which is why they used trees for their horoscope, but these should not be confused with Celtic horoscopes. There are thirteen signs that are each associated with a specific lunar phase.
        - Birch
        - Rowan
        - Ash
        - Alder
        - Willow
        - Hawthorn

        - Oak
        - Hazel
        - Vine
        - Ivy
        - Cane
        - Elder
- Egyptian Horoscopes
    - Egyptian horoscopes went off of the deep motivations of an individual, and their horoscopes are based on lunar cycles but are named after the different Egyptian Gods.
        - Osiris
        - Isis
        - Thot
        - Anubis
        - Seth
        - Horus
        - Sekhmet
        - Bastet
        - Geb
        - Nout
        - Amon Ray
        - Hapi

- Gypsy Horoscope
    - The gypsy tribes are distinguished based on their roaming arts like divinity and palm reading, so it is only natural that they developed their own horoscope. They are broken down by twelve signs that are dependent upon the date of birth.
        - Cup
        - Chapel
        - Dagger
        - Crown
        - Candlesticks
        - Wheel
        - Star
        - Bell
        - Coin
        - Knife
        - Ax
        - Horseshoe
- Native American Horoscope
    - There are again, twelve animal signs that are indicative of the region in which they frequent on occasion.
        - Snow Goose

        - Woodpecker
        - Otter
        - Sturgeon
        - Puma
        - Brown Bear
        - Hawk
        - Raven
        - Beaver
        - Snake
        - Stag
        - Moose
- Mayan Horoscope
    - The Mayan calendar was broken down into twenty-day months, which gave them a total of thirteen signs.
        - Tzootz-Bat
        - Dzec-Scorpion
        - Keh-Deer
        - Moan-Owl
        - Kutz-Peacock
        - Kibray-Lizard
        - Batz Kimil-Monkey
        - Coz-Hawk
        - Balam-Jaguar

        - Fex-Dog
        - Kan-Snake
        - Tzub-Rabbit
        - Aak-Turtle
- Orisha Horoscope
    - The Cuban religion, Yoruba, has twelve signs that are named for the deities.
        - Ogun
        - Oko
        - Elegua
        - Oshun
        - Shango
        - Yemanya
        - Obatala
        - Orula
        - Babalu Aye
        - Agayu Sola
        - Oshosi
        - Inle
- Wuyku Horoscope
    - This is an ancient Tibetan horoscope that only has four signs. These are represented by animals held sacred by the Buddhists.

Each one represents three months of the calendar year.

- Spider
- Ant
- Scorpion
- Turtle

Vedic Astrology

Vedic astrology is the traditional study of astrology in India. It is also known as Hindu astrology. It has only more recently been called Vedic astrology because of ancient Vedic texts that were unearthed regarding the astrological history in India.

Astrology is an important part of Hindu culture. Newborns are traditionally named based on their birth chart and where their birth falls on it. They also believe the same as Western astrology, that many things can be told about a person based on their signs and the position of the planets when they were born. The only difference is that the Hindu believes it to be a fixed system, one that does not move, whereas Western cultures believe that it rotates around the Earth.

The Hindu culture believes in a system of lunar mansions (nakastras), which are equivalent to the twelve houses in Western astrology. In ancient Hindu culture, there were twenty-eight, but the list was reduced to twenty-seven.

- Ashvini
- Krittika
- Bharni
- Mrighashirsha
- Rohini
- Punarvasu
- Ardra
- Pushya
- Magha
- Aslesha
- Uttara Phalguni
- Purva Phalguni
- Chitra
- Hasta
- Vishakha
- Swati
- Jyeshtha
- Anuradha
- Purva Ashada

- Moola
- Shravana
- Uttara Ashada
- Dhanishta
- Purva Bhadrapada
- Shatabhishak
- Uttara Bhadrapada
- Revati

Impact on Daily Life

Opening up the newspaper and reading your horoscope is only a generalization of how your day could go. You may find out that today may be a particularly bad day for your zodiac sign, but that doesn't necessarily mean that you will have a bad day yourself. This just means that an astrologer has concluded that for this given birth sign, based on indicators, they could possibly have a bad day. Personalized horoscopes are a little more in-depth. They start with your exact birth date and pinpoint planets at the given time you are seeking answers to. The only way to get an accurate foreshadowing of events would be to get a personalized reading. This isn't to discredit the newspapers printing the generalized horoscopes, though; there is a lot of factors to obtain when looking to get information based on your own life. The generalized ones should be taken with a grain of salt, and used as a guideline, but not a truth.

Astrology and horoscopes can tell you a lot about yourself, though. Personalized readings are more accurate. They explain things like your personality, your successes, your failures, and your relationships. Each sign has unique attributes, which will be discussed further in a later chapter. Even though some want to try to discredit the accuracy of using astrology as a science, there are just too many coincidences in the readings to be considered unscientific. That is why you will find that the line between astrology and astronomy is often thin.

Influence in the Field of Astronomy

Astronomy is the natural science that studies the phenomena and celestial objects in space. This uses chemistry, mathematics, and physics to explain changes in the atmosphere as well as the origin and evolution of the planets and stars. Cosmology, which is a branch of astronomy, explores and studies the Universe as a whole entity.

As a profession, astronomy is broken into two sectors. The first sector is observational astronomy. In observational astronomy, astronomers focus on the things that they can observe and explain. They analyze their data using physics. The other sector is theoretical astronomy. In theoretical astronomy, astronomers use computer models to describe astronomical events. These two branches work hand in hand. Theoretical astronomy helps describe the organizational finds, and the organizational finds help fuel the theoretical ones.

There is a crossover between the field of astronomy and astrology. Both recognize the celestial and cosmic bodies, or the stars and planets. The only difference is how each science interprets the data. Even the names of the stars and planets remain the same.

Impact of Astronomy on Daily Life

There are a lot of things in our everyday life that astronomy has touched and influenced that we don't even realize. The most commonly used advantage of astronomy in daily life is the wireless local area network (WLAN). Other advantages that astronomy has paved the way for are observatory x-ray technology. This is currently used in airports for their luggage belts in order to ensure that things concealed in baggage are safe. Police officers use hand-held devices called chemical oxygen demand photometers that allow them to check the transparency of vehicle windows to ensure they are transparent enough and up to code. A gamma-ray spectrometer that was originally created to analyze lunar soil is now being used as a way to look into the structures of historic buildings without damaging them.

The original calendars were synced with the movements of the moon. Time, down to the second, is synchronized with outer space. The atomic clock that was developed in 1955 was calibrated using astronomy. This led to what defined the time increment of a second internationally.

First NPL atomic clock with Essen (r) and Parry (1955). Original photo from papers of L. Essen.

Astronomy has brought forth International liaisons of its own. The cost of space stations is high, and it is better to share the cost and get the vantage points from various views than to go in debt on your own. All of the current astronomical

liaisons thus far have been extremely peaceful and highly profitable for all the parties involved.

Why the Surge in Popularity?

The first real surge in horoscopic popularity was right after the stock market crashed. A story was published with the horoscope of the Princess Margaret. This brought forth a diversion for the masses who were scared of their current situations. After the nineteen seventies, though, they seem to have fizzled out. Some believe that it is because of the decline in organized religious views. Here recently, political issues that have risen along with other uncertainty in people's lives have caused them to turn to something to believe in.

Not only are newspapers using astrologers to post in their papers, but other marketing campaigns are embarking on this venture as well. Stores are beginning to hire astrologers to help customers forecast their need for certain goods. This is something that is somewhat hard to believe, mainly because millennials are the hardest generation to please on things that come to beliefs. They are the surging popularity though on the rehashed horoscope business.

People are trying to reconnect to the roots of those that came before us. It is quite possible that the past political references that used astrology are being revisited by the public and seem to be a beacon of hope in this mixed-up world we are living in. People are seeking out something to believe in to get them through tough times and make sense of things, even if it is a future that has been depicted through the stars and planets.

Chapter 2: Zodiac Signs

The zodiac was originally a term that was coined by the Greeks. They interpreted it as a "circle of animals," which is where it got its name. This zodiac is comprised of twelve segments, each with its own corresponding star constellation. Since then, the twelve have also been broken down further. Each zodiac sign now belongs to an element, modality, and ruler planet. These have a lot of influence on the characteristics exerted by someone falling under a specific sign.

Qualities (Modalities)

There are three modalities, also called qualities that the zodiac signs fall under. Each of the qualities have their own characteristics, which are brought out by their elemental force, which is why you will not see more than one quality per element. Because of this, it is often easier for opposite signs to bridge gaps because they tend to share the same qualities.

Cardinal

Cardinal qualities rule over all the other qualities; they are leaders and are open to new things. Each of the cardinal qualities is the beginning of a new season and this is why they are defined as being new and innovative.

Fixed

Fixed qualities are the calm after the storm. They are that still point in the middle of the season where it is clearly defined. Fixed signs find change hard to cope with and are usually firmly set in their ways.

Mutable

Mutable signs are the ones that get bored and want change. They can't wait for the seasons to change, and they are a mixture of the old and the new qualities of both. It is believed that those with a mutable quality are clairvoyant.

Fire Signs

The signs under the fire element are Aries, Sagittarius, and Leo. Fire is considered to be the first of the elements that was born. Fire is also synonymous with passion, energy, and creation. The fire signs can be tricky. Depending on the energies that are tapped into, the signs can become impatient and quick-tempered, or they can be confident and passionate. The individual characteristics of each fire sign will be broken down further based on the zodiac.

Aries

Dates: March 21-April 20

About: Aries is the first sign in the zodiac. It is interpreted from Latin to mean "ram."

Strengths: Confident, optimistic, passionate, courageous, enthusiastic, determined, honest

Weaknesses: Moody, impulsive, impatient, aggressive, short-tempered

Quality: Cardinal

Ruling Planet: Mars

Likes: Physical challenges, comfortable clothing, individual sports, leadership roles

Dislikes: Work that does not exhibit one's talents, inactivity, delays in anything

Aries Men: Aries men are a rare breed. They are always very sure of themselves, mentally and physically. These men have very little patience for a partner who is insecure or lacks confidence. When showing appreciation for yourself, as well as him, the Aries man is a tiger in the sheets.

Unfortunately, a relationship with an Aries man may never develop more than a romp in the sheets. They are proven to be chauvinistic and would rather be alone than taking care of someone else. If you fall in love with an Aries man, you better be stable in all areas if it is going to work.

When an Aries man does fall in love, he can fall on two different ends of the spectrum. He will either fight hard for it, or he will be so unsure of what his emotions are doing that he will lose touch with reality and shy away from it.

Aries Women: Do not take an Aries woman for granted. She is fierce and loves hard when she falls. She is not like a typical woman, and it is important to remember that. To avoid conflict, allow her to work her emotions out on her own and in her own time. She can come across aggressive and loud but that is just her personality and should be appreciated.

Aries women know that they are attractive and will tastefully show it, no matter how short the skirt or low the shirt. She finds it inappropriate to stay in a relationship that does not satisfy her sexually. When she is in love, though, she will always be faithful and support her partner in all of their plans and dreams.

Aries women are some of the most trustworthy when it comes to women in the zodiac. They prefer to constantly move forward, without dwelling on the past. When the past creeps in, for whatever reason, they have trouble processing it, and it can cause problems for them.

Most Compatible: Leo and Libra

Leo

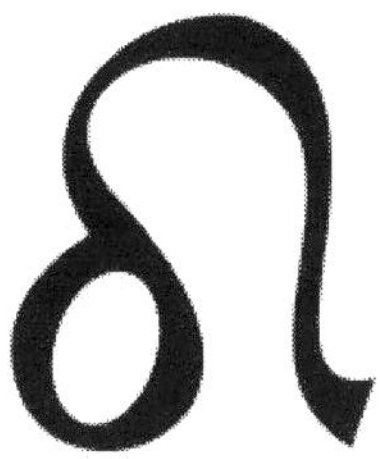

Dates: July 23-August 22

About: The translation for Leo means "lion." Those under the Leo sign are kings of the jungle, so to speak.

Strengths: Generous, creative, cheerful, passionate, humorous, warm-hearted

Weaknesses: Stubborn, inflexible, arrogant, lazy, self-centered

Quality: Fixed

Ruling Planet: Sun

Likes: Being admired, bright colors, taking vacations, expensive things, theater, having fun with their friends

Dislikes: Not being treated like the royalty they think that they are, being ignored, facing difficult realities around them

Leo Men: The fixed sign of Leo can make it hard for a Leo man when it comes to relationships. He has trouble letting old relationships go, which can cause problems when pursuing new relationships. Leo men enjoy the chase of their "prey" and is driven by the seduction period. This can cause problems for them, though, they come across as lazy and bossy, which can make them seem like they only see themselves as the center of the Universe.

A big step to understanding a Leo man is that he is not secretive; he just prefers to keep things that are of serious nature, especially his feelings to himself. As the "king," he doesn't want to show weakness to those he cares about. He wants to protect those around him, even if it means he has to make compromises. For this alone, Leo men should have respect.

Leo Women: Despite the self-involved description of the Leo personality, when a Leo woman falls in love, she makes her partner the center of her Universe. When the Leo woman knows what she wants, she won't stop until she gets it. Leo women do have the potential to be called high-maintenance in relationships, but this is dependent on their past and upbringing.

Leo women are often classified as grumpy or unsatisfied. Her outspoken nature often clouds the judgment of those around her, but the truth of the matter is she is generally just making us face the things that we are not comfortable facing. If you are not willing to face things, then chances are you should not be around Leo women.

Compatibility: Gemini and Aquarius

Sagittarius

Dates: November 22-December 21

About: The Sagittarius sign is the biggest wanderer out of all the zodiac. They are the traveling sign.

Strengths: Great sense of humor, generous, idealistic

Weaknesses: Will say whatever no matter how blunt, impatient, promises more than can be delivered

Quality: Mutable

Ruling Planet: Jupiter

Likes: Philosophy, freedom, being outside, traveling

Dislikes: Details, being constrained, people who are clingy, off-the-wall theories

Sagittarius Men: These men are quick to fall in love. It is important to keep him at a distance, though until you know what his intentions are. He will enjoy starting a relationship on a whim but will only stay fascinated if there is something for him to fight for. He is not necessarily reliable in a relationship though. He has a mutable quality which makes him ready for change constantly. He does not want to get bored in a relationship. Therefore, it is hard to tell how he will feel in the coming hours, days, or weeks.

He is an adventurous man, but he doesn't always understand why. He can come across as childish at times, but this is just how his nature is misconstrued. He is full of adventure, but even if he makes reckless decisions, he knows when it is time to stop. When he finds "the one," that is the only time he will fully stop and settle down. He will feel as if all of his questions have been answered and he has found the truth he has been searching for.

Sagittarius Women: Sagittarius women fall in love fast. They may not even be feeling the true feelings of love, but they pursue them full force. She is always searching for human contact that can make her feel complete, which makes her easily tricked by those who are deceiving. She is naïve, though, and she believes there is goodness in everyone. She makes it her own personal goal to make everyone happy around her. This can make her come across as slightly childish in nature, but in truth, it is her good spirits coming through. Her love life is a mess, but not because of the relationship. She is a very clumsy being in the bedroom. She can laugh at herself and is looking for you to take it for what it is too, and not be supercritical.

The Sagittarius woman wants to make the lives of those around her better. She does have the habit of pushing her own opinions onto people, which can become easily irritating, but know she does it with the best of intentions. Her ultimate goal is to make the world a better place, but in order for her to remain realistic, she needs for her beliefs and dreams not to be crushed and remain intact.

Compatibility: Aries and Gemini

Air Signs

The Air signs of the zodiac are Gemini, Libra, and Aquarius. These signs often have a hard time fitting into the regular order of things. Those under the element of air prefer to be free and liberated from the general status quo. These signs will not do what they need to in order to please others; they want to follow their own paths and do not worry about the opinions of others either.

It is easy for those under the Air element to become off their given course. They need to have balance in their life and often look to those of the Earth element to satisfy it. They can become unreasonable and "in the clouds" if they do not tend to their personal needs, which they are known to forget about quite often.

Gemini

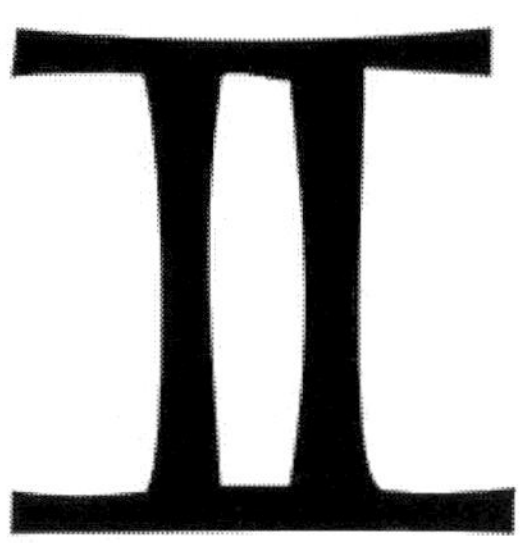

Dates: May 21-June 21

About: Gemini is the sign of the "twin." The Gemini often exhibit two personalities in one person.

Strengths: Curious, gentle, ability to learn quickly, affectionate, adaptable

Weaknesses: Indecisive, inconsistent, nervous

Quality: Mutable

Ruling Planet: Mercury

Likes: Books, short trips, talking to people, music, magazines

Dislikes: Repetition, being confined, being alone, routine

Gemini Men: You cannot expect consistency with a Gemini man. Their mutable quality has them constantly looking for a change in their life. He is unsure of his feelings because he lives in the moment, and if for a moment, he feels that he is in love, he will take it on with full force. He needs a partner who is willing to change as he changes and can handle the spontaneous compulsions in his life. Think of this man as a year of seasons. He is new in spring, hot in summer, homely in the fall, and cold and distant in the winter. This will become the revolving door of his emotions.

The only way to truly understand a Gemini man is to find the burning core of his heart. He does not understand his own emotions, so this might be a hard task. This is especially difficult if he has been hurt in the past because his guarded emotions outreach to even himself. If you can reach him and his inner core, you will find an innocence that is almost childish in nature, but a true reflection of his inner beauty. This will be something that no one else will see.

Gemini Women: Gemini women are known to fall out of love just as quickly as they fell into it. They like for relationships to be exciting and new all of the time and will not stay in a relationship that does not make them happy. Making a Gemini woman happy can be a complicated thing, though. She knows what she is looking for, but at the same time, needs to have the freedom to fly and explore. She will not thrive in an environment where she is "tied down," which makes her wither away and lose her shine if she is in a relationship with someone who is possessive.

The sign of the Gemini typically controls speech; however, a Gemini will not talk endlessly for days. If your Gemini woman is speaking in excess, it is because she wants to be heard, and it is something that matters deeply to her. She seeks change but is reasonable in doing so. She thinks things through, even if it does not look as though she has. She needs someone true in human nature to satisfy her in life.

Compatibility: Aquarius and Sagittarius

Libra

Dates: September 24-October 23

About: Those born under the sign of the Libra are often balanced in life and look for symmetry in the things they do. They are constantly chasing justice in the inequality around them.

Strengths: Fair-minded, diplomatic, social, cooperative, gracious

Weaknesses: Carries grudges, indecisive, pities themselves, avoidance of confrontations

Quality: Cardinal

Ruling Planet: Venus

Likes: Sharing with other people, harmony, being outside, gentleness

Dislikes: Injustice, conformity, violence, loud-mouthed people

Libra Men: Libra men fall fast, and they fall hard. They will be the first one to bring up marriage and usually early on. They do not want to waste time on something if it isn't going to turn into something long term. This is to their demise, though because they will constantly try to fix everything in their lives as well as their partner's lives. Sometimes this comes at a great cost for them. Libra men can often end up used because their feelings are all in. If they have been hurt in the past, they can often come across childish until they are shown that they can trust a new partner.

Libra men are men of mystery. He carries the weight of the world on his shoulders, literally. He feels the immense need to find balance and justice in everything that comes his way. When he has taken on too much, he cannot break free from this burden until he realizes that he needs to be alone to self-evaluate and start fresh.

Libra Women: Libra women question their decision to be in love like it is something they can control. She will do all of the things she can to fall out of love with someone she sees as being unacceptable to her standards. She wants to be liberal but is often more into traditional values and views. When she is with someone, she is committed and loyal to them but be prepared because she will not be willing to let out her uncontrolled emotions freely. She will remain reserved until she has complete comfort in her feelings.

The Libra woman will often find herself in a state of self-pity and being the victim. She has low self-esteem, which plays the primary role in her view of herself. She cannot comprehend why people do not act the way she would in certain situations, which causes her to second guess herself. She cares too much about what others think, which can make her hard to be around at times.

Compatibility: Sagittarius and Aries

Aquarius

Dates: January 21-February 19

About: Those born under the sign of Aquarius are deep thinkers and often easily solve problems. They adapt easily and often see the world as being full of possibilities.

Strengths: Independent, progressive, humanitarian, original

Weaknesses: Fail to compromise in situations, run away from emotional expression, aloof, temperamental

Quality: Fixed

Ruling Planet: Saturn and Uranus

Likes: Helping others, conversations that intelligent, having fun with friends, fighting for a cause, a good listener

Dislikes: Being lonely, people who do not see things the way they see them, boring situations, broken promises, limitations

Aquarius Men: Aquarius men are often hard to read. He has a lot of trouble communicating how he feels, and this will be the case until he feels that you are worthy of the information. He has to be in tune with his inner feelings, which can trigger him to go into a darker place that seems unnecessarily negative at times. Aquarius men tend to take things that are said to them, too personally. He will not end up hurt by these feelings, but instead, he will feel more disrespected. It is important to set clear boundaries at the start of a relationship with a man born under the Aquarius sign.

Aquarius men are known for their talent and strong beliefs, even if he will keep them hidden. He will more than likely always be late to anywhere he needs to be. His dignified attitude will come across as distant because you will be kept at arms-length until your worthiness has been assessed. If he does let you in, be prepared to see his inner heart.

Aquarius Women: Aquarius women can follow two courses in the same lifetime. They are wild and free until they find the one that they fall madly in love with. That is when the Aquarius woman will change her ways and settle down to marry and have children. It is important to remember, though, that while this may be a normalized occurrence, for the Aquarius woman, this is a huge deal. She will only allow herself to become tied down for the right person in life. She also has to remain feeling that she can be herself or it will never work.

Aquarius women fight an internal battle regarding self-respect. She will always tell herself that respect is something that has to be earned and may never allow herself to fully feel the respect she is given. She is challenged by finding her own inner peace, and if she is hurt, she can easily close her heart and move on.

Compatibility: Sagittarius and Leo

Water Signs

The zodiac signs that fall under the element of Water are Cancer, Scorpio, and Pisces. The water element is the element of emotions and can encompass the matters of life and death. These emotions are generally passed from generation to generation through the family tree, generally by a female. Water signs have it hard because they have the role of embracing all the emotions. They have to be able to process the negative and the positive, the anger and the sadness, the happiness, and the love. The water signs are an endless element with the greatest of possibilities, but they have so much trouble expressing themselves creatively it is hard to see it.

Cancer

Dates: June 22-July 22

About: Cancer signs are often loyal to those they love. The sign of the Cancer zodiac is the crab, which is an animal that does not know its own strength. This is much like the ones who are born under the sign.

Strengths: Highly imaginative, sympathetic, loyal, persuasive, tenacious, emotional

Weaknesses: Suspicious, insecure, moody, manipulative, pessimistic

Quality: Cardinal

Ruling Planet: Moon

Likes: Helping loved ones, home-based hobbies, sharing a meal with friends, relaxing near water, art

Dislikes: Revealing their personal life, strangers, criticism

Cancer Men: A man born under the sign of Cancer can be full of insecurities about himself, and they can rise up quickly, hitting him like a ton of bricks. He is sensitive to the person he is with and will make them the center of his life. He will never forget an important date, but he will be cautious and afraid of opening up. He can stay calm in the craziest of situations and most other zodiac signs find him boring.

Cancer men often come across as being too sensitive. He may seem weak because of this, but he is quite the opposite. There is a good chance that he is constantly judged by people he brings into his life, so he may be more reserved when opening up his sensitive side. You can tell so much about a man born under this sign by the relationship that he has with his mother.

Cancer Women: Women who are born under the sign of Cancer are generally selfless beings. They will give all to their partners, even if it means they are unsatisfied themselves. She is a giver, and it makes her vulnerable to being used in all kinds of relationships. She has a lot of trouble controlling her motherly instincts and this can often confuse her in relationships.

Because of her Cardinal roots, she will make it a mission to get change in her life. She is considered very strong and ready to give her life in the place of the ones that she loves. She may come across as soft, don't let that fool you. She is a fierce fighter when she needs to be, and she is not someone you want to take on as an enemy.

Compatibility: Taurus and Capricorn

Scorpio

Dates: October 24-November 22

About: The zodiac sign of Scorpio has representation of the scorpion. Scorpios are passionate and decisive and are intent on always finding out the truth. This can make them seem jealous or suspicious most of the time.

Strengths: Brave, stubborn, resourceful, believes in true friendships, passionate

Weaknesses: Jealous, violent, distrustful, secretive

Quality: Fixed

Ruling Planet: Mars and Pluto

Likes: Being right, teasing, facts and truths, passion, lifelong friendships

Dislikes: People who are passive, dishonesty, people who reveal secrets or having to reveal them themselves

Scorpio Men: Men who are born under the sign of Scorpio can be summed up with the word "intense." They get attached to someone and can often scare them away because of their immediate closeness to them. When they think that they have found their true love, they are not quick to let it go and if they do the feeling will often turn to hate rather than disappear. On the flip side of this, he is also a very compassionate man with an incredible sense of emotional understanding. These men can be possessive and obsessive though, but they are loyal and supportive which is why they entrust the one they love with their inner sensitivity and feelings.

The best way to understand a Scorpio man is to understand his emotions fully. Most of the time, they will surround themselves with other Water signs because of the connection, but the best for grounding them are Earth signs. He is on the hunt for the person he will spend the rest of his life with and if you are not the one, expect the relationship to end before it ever really started.

Scorpio Women: Scorpio women let it be known what their intentions are from the start. They do not tease unless they are interested in taking things to the next level, and in most cases, she has already become emotionally invested in you. Be warned though, if she is already emotionally invested and you hurt her, she will become your worst enemy. Scorpio women are passionate, and this can come from love or hate. She needs her partner to be able to speak without using words. She is a bottle of emotions that have been held in for a long time and she needs to be able to express herself without blowing the top off the bottle.

Scorpio women come across as hard to handle, but that is from their need to know exactly what they want and where they are going in life. This is so that they do not become unhinged by the emotions that flow freely through their bodies. She does not accept what she is feeling free, and she will try to divert her focus from things she truly loves to harness it.

Compatibility: Cancer and Taurus

Pisces

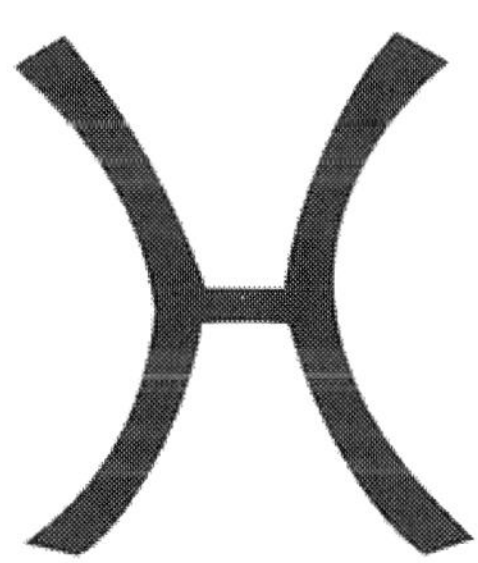

Dates: February 20-March 20

About: Pisces are shown as the "fish" on the traditional zodiac. They are characterized by being selfless and always willing to help others. Those under this sign tend to be more artistic and intuitive.

Strengths: Artistic, gentle, compassionate, wise, intuitive, musical

Weaknesses: Trust too much, can be seen as a victim or martyr, seek escape from their reality, fearful, sad

Quality: Mutable

Ruling Planet: Jupiter and Neptune

Likes: Sleeping, romance, swimming, visual media arts, spirituality, being alone

Dislikes: Being criticized, cruelty, the past haunting them, know-it-all types

Pisces Men: Men born under the Pisces sign tend to care more about what other men think and will use their adaptive advantage to blend in with them. Pisces men have many loves in their lifetime and will love each one with their whole heart until they realize that the person they are with is not what they were looking for to complete them. This can lead to Pisces men having the reputation of infidelity, being dishonest, and constantly trying to find himself.

These men set a lot of personal goals for themselves and often feel a lot of inner disappointment when they do not achieve them. They are loners by default and need time to themselves to reflect. They may seem engaged in a social setting, but do not let their adaptive nature fool you. They need to be able to express themselves to get their creativity that bottles up in them out in the open.

Pisces Women: Pisces women are driven by the uncertainty of things. They will remain in relationships, believing that they are with "the one," for as long as the end seems uncertain to them. They are highly emotional beings and will be drained by the rational moments in life that she must come into contact with, but don't worry because it is her emotions and childish nature that will recharge her and give her plenty of energy to carry on. She will often keep her partner in the friendzone for a longer period of time than other signs because she enjoys the possibilities over the actual outcomes.

Pisces women have "daddy issues." Either their fathers were not present in their life to their needing, or they were over-idealized individuals. Either way, she is looking for someone who can fill the shoes, which is almost always difficult for someone to do. The only way she works past this is to have her own purpose, which means to love her, you mustn't let anything get in her way of achieving the things she needs to achieve to feel complete and understood.

Compatibility: Taurus and Virgo

Earth Signs

The zodiac signs that are classified under the element of Earth are Taurus, Virgo, and Capricorn. These signs are practical signs and lay more importance on physical things versus anything else. The element of Earth is important because all things need to connect back to the soil from which they come from. One of the biggest challenges that Earth signs deal with is the idea of change. Air elements are absolutely frightening to the Earthly elements. This is why something that breaks up the day for them, unplanned, should happen so that they can break the monotony of their day.

Taurus

Dates: April 21-May 21

About: The zodiac sign of Taurus is the bull. Much like its name, it is stubborn and very well content on sticking to its path in life until they have achieved something to the point of personal satisfaction.

Strengths: Practical, reliable, responsible, patient, stable

Weaknesses: Uncompromising, possessive, stubborn

Quality: Fixed

Ruling Planet: Venus

Likes: Music, gardening, romance, cooking, working with their hands, nice clothing

Dislikes: Complications, synthetic fabrics, sudden changes in life or around them, insecurities

Taurus Men: For lack of better terms, Taurus men can be lazy when it comes to confronting their feelings. There is a panic that creeps up in them when they are forced to look into their own desires and feelings, and they will back away slowly. If they are the ones to make the first move when it comes to their feelings, it is because they have carefully thought about the situation for a long time and are confident in what they are feeling. Taurus men tend to go through a phase where they don't want to do anything. This is a complication of their personality type, and the only way to combat this is to keep them moving. Even if it is for a short walk around the block, it is important for the Taurus man to go outside at least once a day, especially if he is in that phase.

These men tend to be aware of their sensitivity, which is why they feel such a need to hide it. They see it as being weak, but in reality, it is his biggest attribute. He does have the ability to be spontaneous, but don't bank on it being very often.

Taurus Women: Taurus women are the most rounded women of the zodiac. They have the ability to be your cook, your mother, and your lover, all at once without any of the lines blurring together. She is a woman of sensuality and wants to be stimulated on that level instead of sexually. Because of her deep fear of getting hurt, it is important to allow her to gradually build her trust in you so that she can allow you into her heart completely.

In order to understand a woman born under the Taurus sign, you need to understand her emotions. You have to be gentle with her and feel her emotionally and mentally. She is compassionate to a fault that can make her the target for those looking to use someone.

Compatibility: Cancer and Scorpio

Virgo

Dates: August 23-September 23

About: The zodiac sign of Virgo represents "the virgin." Those born under this sign generally show the emotion of feeling things for the first time. They often don't accept these feelings either, which makes them the most careful of all the zodiac signs.

Strengths: Kind, loyal, practical, analytical, hardworking

Weaknesses: Overly critical of themselves and others, shy, believe in all work and no play philosophy, excessive worry

Quality: Mutable

Ruling Planet: Earth

Likes: Books, cleanliness, healthy foods, nature, animals

Dislikes: Taking center stage, rudeness, having to ask someone else for help

Virgo Men: Virgo men follow a strict moral compass. He can be seen as a man who is very pleasing or a man who is very annoying. He prefers to keep his true emotions a secret but isn't going to let go of the one he loves. He will, however, find a new love if his current one does not live up to the expectations that he holds for them. Despite having these strict expectations for his partner, he is very insecure about the emotions he feels for himself. If a Virgo man has trust issues, it is strongly probably they stem from his own dishonesty.

Virgo men have an insatiable need to fix things. They do not feel satisfied in life unless they have fixed all the things they need to fix; this includes their partner. If you do not allow him to be the fixer, he will let you know all of the things you have broken by your own hands. It is easier to let a Virgo fix the situation.

Virgo Women: Virgo women need to be swept off of their feet. They do not want to be the ones to make the first move in situations. They are scared by the idea of falling in love, but if they are pursued by a partner who is more confident, protective, and confident then they are, they are likely to pursue them back. Much like the Virgo man, she will try to be a fixer. She takes this to a whole different level, though. She will try to make herself useful in all areas of life and will more than likely take on too much in the process. It is better to let her know that she doesn't have to do everything herself because, without that guidance, she has no shut off in her brain to do it herself.

Virgo women have the tendency to be cleaners. This can be from the principle that Virgo women want to clean evil from the world. They do not see themselves as a worthy person, and this makes them need to find something to believe in. The worst thing for her is to settle with rational thoughts, especially if she is seeking to perfect her life.

Compatibility: Cancer and Pisces

Capricorn

Dates: December 22-January 20

About: The Capricorn zodiac has the head of a goat, but the tail of a fish. This sign is serious in nature and is synonymous with time and responsibility. Capricorns are also notorious for resisting change and imposing their traditional values on those around them.

Strengths: Disciplined, managerial, responsible, good with self-control

Weaknesses: Always expect the worst, unforgiving, know-it-all attitude, condescending at times

Quality: Cardinal

Ruling Planet: Saturn

Likes: Music, family, quality craftmanship, traditions

Dislikes: At some point in their lives, they dislike everything

Capricorn Men: Capricorn men prefer to keep their emotions to themselves, mainly because they don't understand them. Despite this characteristic, he is the most stable and deeply emotional sign in the zodiac. He does not regard anything lightly and refuses to be superficial with anything, which makes his deeply rooted emotions worth it once they surface. He can be seen as possessive with high expectations, and this may be true until he finds the true love that can melt his heart and strip away his insecurities.

These men are afraid of failure and are way too strict on themselves. Because of this, he comes across cold and distant and rational to a fault. He is overly cautious because he does not want to have to deal with karma and will build his walls high and thick to prevent outside things from controlling his life.

Capricorn Women: Capricorn women are methodical when it comes to love. They like to explore their feelings before acting upon them. They feel a huge sense of responsibility that does not allow them to take risks, so all moves must be seriously calculated. She will always choose the safe plan, even if it costs her happiness. This can often lead to her making sure that she does not disappoint and will not leave. The only thing that can cause a Capricorn woman to flee is fear or panic. If she is scared or panicking about the situation or she has just plain had enough, she will run, and she won't look back. Capricorn women live to take care of others, even to their own detriment. What this means is that she will sacrifice all things about herself to take care of those around her. She feels an insane need to do this, especially if she is feeling guilty about something. Most times, this guilt is something she has placed in her head herself with the need to atone for it.

Compatibility: Cancer and Taurus

Chinese Zodiac

The Chinese zodiac is based on the year you were born though the execution is different; there are still personality traits that are said to accompany each of the twelve animals that lie within it. These are laid out by Chinese divining science that focuses on the five elements (wood, fire, water, metal, and air), the Yin and the Yang, cycles of time, and Chi.

The story that accompanies this tradition is that when Buddha was departing from Earth, he called upon the animals to give him his farewell. Only twelve of these animals came, and they are memorialized by having a year dedicated to them. That is why each animal runs on a twelve-year cycle in the Chinese zodiac.

These are the same novelty horoscopes that you see on your placemat at your favorite Chinese buffet. These are just as accurate as the regular zodiac at describing the attributes of a person, only it is based on birth year and not a specific birth date and time.

<u>Rat</u>

Years: 1900, 1912, 1924, 1936, 1948, 1960, 1972, 1984, 1996, 2008, 2020

Characteristics: Adaptable, charming, sociable, intelligent, quick-witted, artistic

Element: Water

Partners: Monkey and Dragon

<u>Ox/Bull</u>

Years: 1901, 1913, 1925, 1937, 1949, 1961, 1973, 1985, 1997, 2009, 2021

Characteristics: Reliable, strong, loyal, reasonable, determined, steady, thorough

Element: Earth

Partners: Rooster and Snake

<u>Tiger</u>

Years: 1902, 1914, 1926, 1938, 1950, 1962, 1974, 1986, 1998, 2010, 2022

Characteristics: Courageous, leader, charisma, enthusiasm, ambition, confident

Element: Wood

Partners: Dog and Horse

Rabbit

Years: 1903, 1915, 1927, 1939, 1951, 1963, 1975, 1987, 1999, 2011, 2023

Characteristics: Modest, caretakers, trustworthy, sincere, empathetic, social, diplomatic, sensitive

Element: Wood

Partners: Pig/Boar and Goat/Sheep

Dragon

Years: 1904, 1916, 1928, 1940, 1952, 1964, 1976, 1988, 2000, 2012, 2024

Characteristics: Flexible, imaginative, lucky, charismatic, artistic, eccentric, spiritual

Element: Earth

Partners: Monkey and Rat

Snake

Years: 1905, 1917, 1929, 1941, 1953, 1965, 1977, 1989, 2001, 2013, 2025

Characteristics: Organized, intuitive, elegant, decisive, philosophical, attentive, intelligent

Element: Fire

Partners: Ox/Bull and Rooster

Horse

Years: 1906, 1918, 1930, 1942, 1954, 1966, 1978, 1990, 2002, 2014, 2026

Characteristics: Ambitious, loyal, intelligent, adaptable, strong, courageous, adventurous

Element: Fire

Partners: Tiger and Dog

Goat/Sheep

Years: 1907, 1919, 1931, 1943, 1955, 1967, 1979, 1991, 2003, 2015, 2027

Characteristics: Warm, charming, tasteful, intuitive, crafty, calm, sensitive

Element: Earth

Partners: Rabbit and Pig/Boar

Monkey

Years: 1908, 1920, 1932, 1944, 1956, 1968, 1980, 1992, 2004, 2016, 2028

Characteristics: Adaptable, quick-witted, bright, charming, lively, lucky, smart

Element: Metal

Partners: Rat and Dragon

Rooster

Years: 1909, 1921, 1933, 1945, 1957, 1969, 1981, 1993, 2005, 2017, 2029

Characteristics: Flamboyant, honest, diverse, energetic, confident, intelligent, flexible

Element: Metal

Partners: Ox/Bull and Snake

Dog

Years: 1910, 1922, 1934, 1946, 1958, 1970, 1982, 1994, 2006, 2018, 2030

Characteristics: Diligent, lively, smart, loyal, adaptive, courageous, steady, sociable

Element: Earth

Partners: Horse and Tiger

Pig/Boar

Years: 1911, 1923, 1935, 1947, 1959, 1971, 1983, 1995, 2007, 2019, 2031

Characteristics: Philanthropic, optimistic, honorable, determined, sociable, sincere

Element: Water

Partners: Rabbit and Goat/Sheep

Interesting Facts About Horoscopes and the Zodiac

Cancer is the Most Dangerous Sign

In data that was compiled by the FBI, they found that the zodiac sign that is most often arrested is Cancer. They also tend to commit more serious crimes.

In Japan, Blood Type Defines Personality, Not Zodiac Signs

Instead of using zodiac signs to assign personality traits to people, in Japan, they use blood type to assign these traits. When getting to know someone from Japanese culture, it is not uncommon for them to ask your blood type in general conversation.

Billionaires Are Aries

When Forbes conducted a list of billionaires, the analysis concluded that more billionaires were born under the sign of the ram than any other zodiac sign. It is thought that people under this sign are more determined, and that is the reason behind it.

A Pope Drew Up a Horoscope

Christianity and horoscopes have not been subjects that mix very well. The Christian faith does not acknowledge astrology as a science, but in the fifteenth century, Pope Sixtus IV was the first pope to make and interpret his own horoscope.

The Zodiac Was Used for Farming

The original use of the zodiac was almost in the way a present-day almanac was used. The people would use the zodiac to know when to plant, when to harvest, and to predict the weather patterns by using the constellations and their movements.

There is an Abandoned Sign

When the Babylonians came up with the twelve-month calendar, the thirteenth sign was abandoned. Ophiuchus was removed because there was no room for it in ancient charts.

Ophiuchus

Gemini Signs Quit More Jobs

Based on the idea that those under the Gemini sign have a dual personality, they are believed to quit their jobs more often.

Americans Believe in Astrology

According to the National Science Foundation, over forty percent of Americans believe in astrology as a science.

Scorpio is the Most Common Sign

People born under the sign of the Scorpion are more common in America than any other sign. It is predicted that this may, or may not, have something to do with the fact that Valentine's Day falls in February. This makes due dates in November.

The Moon Used to be Considered Evil

In Ancient Egypt, they believed that the moon was an evil star. In western civilization, though, the moon plays a very important role.

Your Birth Year is Unlucky

The Chinese zodiac cycles every twelve years and is factored using your birth year. It is a common misconception that this makes your birth year lucky. This is not the case. People are advised that they need to use caution on their birthday that is the multiple of twelve.

Mercury Retrograde Isn't What You Think

When Mercury goes into retrograde, the only change that happens is in its appearance. It appears that it is rotating in the opposite direction, but it is merely an optical illusion.

There Are Thousands of Astrologers in the United States

If you are looking to find a more personal approach to your horoscope and astrological chart, there are over seven thousand documented astrologers currently residing in the United States at the moment.

The Moon is as Important as the Sun

While most people tend to focus on their Sun signs because your Sun sign directly relates to your personality, and when looking at a birth chart, that is typically what people are in search of. The placement of your Moon at birth can say a lot about you as well. The Moon sign relates directly to your emotional side. This explains the way that your subconscious works, which is why some people value it more than the Sun sign.

You Can Get an Astrology Degree

Believe it or not, the popularity of astrology has made it an actual degree program. The Kepler College of Astrological Education is located in Washington state, and you can receive a degree in all things astrology. Then you can add to the number of astrologers in the United States.

Chapter 3: Birth Chart

An astrological birth chart is a map that has been put together to show where all the planets are in their rotation around the Sun, from our current point on Earth at the exact moment of a person's birth. This is also called a natal chart. A reading of this chart can tell a person a lot of things about their life. Strengths and weaknesses in character can be identified, timing for important moves and decisions, and the opportunities for soul growth within a specific person are identified.

Calculating your birth chart calls for some very specific and personal information.

- The date of your birth
- The exact time of your birth
- The exact place of your birth

If you are missing any of the vital information, like place or time, it will be hard to give an accurate reading. The ascendant (rising sign) of your birth cannot be accurately measured. You won't be able to accurately know which of the houses the planets fall into on your chart without this information. However, you can still get a lot of useful information from your birth chart without this information.

An astrologer is going to use the information to look for a few key items from your specific birth chart:

- Which of the twelve houses and which zodiac sign each of the planets lie in on the chart
- Venus, the Moon, and Mars' zodiac signs and the house of love
- Jupiter and where you could be lucky
- Saturn for where you may need to work harder
- The angles formed between two planets
- A grouping of three planets in any given sector which could indicate a heavy concentration on a specific energy
- The elemental balance
- The balance of the qualities in the chart
- The patterns formed by the planets on the chart

The astrologer will take all of this information that has been gathered and tally up a score. This score will help them advise you on what aspects of your life need more concentration and how to equal it all out.

Planetary Connections

The Sun

The Sun is the most important planetary body in your birth chart. The link is masculine and connected to your father. The sun represents your ego, your interests, your vitality, your likes and dislikes in basic terms, what motivates you, and what expresses and identifies you as a person. The Sun gives you the "I am" mindset.

The Moon

The Moon is what controls your emotions, so consequently, the mindset that it implies is the "I feel" concept. If you ever notice people and some of them need more assurance than others, look to their moon sign for the answers. The Moon is the governor of all the representations of intuition, habits, feelings of security, and instincts.

The Moon also rules over all the emotions you try to hide from other people as well. These can be things like anger, jealousy, and fear. You like to keep this side hidden, and it is only shown to those who are closest to you.

Mercury

Mercury rules your curiosity. The mindset given to this planet is "I think." Mercury is your communication style; it is how you learn, what sparks your curiosity, problem-solving skills, and your general interests. Someone who is born during Mercury retrograde is often intuitive and a thinker. They rarely rush before thinking something through. If stationary during your birth, Mercury makes you a talkative thinker.

Venus

The planet, Venus, rules your romantic relationships. The mindset associated with Venus is "I love." Venus plays a big role in who you attract, how you interact socially, how you interpret beauty, what you look for in a partner, and how you spend and earn your money.

If Venus was in retrograde when you were born, you find yourself most comfortable in the company of the people you know. You may have lived a limited financial and love life when you were younger, but as time goes on, you will increase in both areas.

If the planet was stationary during your birth, you are a social butterfly. You revere love as an importance and finding a partner as well. You have the capability of having a successful financial life.

Mars

Mars is about your motivation and your initiative. The association of "I act" is used in the description of a Mars mindset. Mars is your driving force in the areas of confidence, aggression, strength, and stamina, and how much of a risk-taker you are. Mars is also synonymous with your sex drive and what you search for when pursuing one.

When you were born, if Mars was in retrograde, you direct your energy inward so that you can avoid all confrontation. If Mars was stationary, you are all about taking action and going after what you want.

Jupiter

"I grow" is the planetary mindset of Jupiter. This planet is the one that rules your ethical decisions, how you feel about life, what areas you show caution in, where you find your luck at, the areas you want to learn, and what you need to do to gain that knowledge. Jupiter is about searching for truths, which is why it is the best planet for governing law and religion, education, and philosophy.

If you were born while Jupiter was in retrograde, you are a reserved philosopher. If it was stationary, you are outspoken on your point of view and your principles.

Saturn

There is no surprise that Saturn is the governing planet of the Capricorn zodiac. The principle of "I achieve" is what Saturn describes in their lives. Ambition, major life decisions, restrictions, limitations, boundaries, feelings of inadequacy, safety, practicality, and hard work theories are what Saturn fuels in a person. Saturn oversees the achievements in your chart that deal with career, wealth, and business.

If Saturn was in retrograde when you were born, you find yourself solely responsible for your own successes and failures. If it was stationary, you are of a more goal-oriented mind that is set on succeeding.

Uranus

Uranus is about rebellion and seeking out the unexpected. The principle of "I evolve" could not be truer for this planet. This planet is where you stand out from the crowd, what areas you will do the unexpected in, where you will find changes, and encompasses the accidents that can happen in your life. It is the "aha" moment that occurs in your life or when you just know something that has happened. The feeling of déjà vu.

Neptune

Neptune is both inspiration and illusion. "I dream" is a concept that can both be helpful or deceptive. Neptune is the reason for this. It is the all encompassment of illusion and confusion versus imagination and creativity. It is like the devil and the angel sitting on your shoulder at any given time, pushing you toward something. Neptune is also what determines the addictions you may develop in life. Drugs, alcohol, gambling, and any other blind spots that can take you by surprise in your life.

If Neptune was in retrograde when you were born, you might have a higher tendency to try to escape your reality. If it was a stationary planet on your chart, you may be artistic but lack the sense of anything realistic.

Pluto

"I empower" is the Pluto mindset. This is the planet that can help you clear out the old to make way for the new in your life. It helps you understand when you feel powerless and how to take charge of that feeling to find your power. It is representative of how your inner beliefs can change over time but that you can choose the positive over the negative and vice versa. It's in your hands.

Did you notice that Earth does not have a place amongst the planets listed above? Never fear, this was not an accident, but intentional. A birth chart is from the viewpoint of the Earth because you were born on Earth. So basically, the interpretation is that your birth represents Earth on the birth chart.

The Twelve Houses of the Zodiac

Imagine the zodiac as if it were a clock. The clock is divided into twelve equal segments. Inside each of these segments, which is referred to as a house, is a ruling sign. This begins with the first house and then is read counterclockwise around the face of it. Each of these houses foretells specific traits and is interpreted by an astrologer with your birth chart. This can help you find out the obstacles or gifts you may encounter in your life.

1st House-The House of Self

The first house is ruled by the sign of Aries. This house covers all of the "firsts" in your life. This also includes new beginnings in your life. First impressions, new initiatives, leadership, and appearance all fall within this house. The sign that falls just on the cusp of this house is called your ascendant, or rising sign.

2nd House-The House of Value

The second house is ruled by the sign of Taurus. This house covers the subjects of your physical and immediate environment. It is the encompassment of your five senses. This house also rules your self-esteem, income, and money.

3rd House-The House of Communication

The third house is ruled by the sign of Gemini. This house covers the area of communication. This includes, but is not limited to, talking, gadgets, thinking, devices like cell phones and instant messaging. Your communications with other people are included within this house. Your siblings, neighborhood members, teachers, school, and the community affairs you participate in fall under this house as well.

4th House-The House of Home and Family

The fourth house of the zodiac is ruled by Cancer and is situated at the bottom of the "clockface." This makes it the house that is the foundation of all things in your life. This is your home, your security, your privacy, your nurturing, and your ability for loving and caring for those you take care of.

5th House-The House of Pleasure

The fifth house is ruled by the sign of Leo. This is the dramatic house on the wheel. Your self-expression, color, creativity, fun, romance, drama, and the attention you give all come from this house. Think of it as the theatre of the zodiac wheel.

6th House-The House of Health

The sixth house is ruled by the sign of Virgo. This is the center point for all things that are health and domain related. Your schedule you keep, how organized you are, your diet, your exercise, what routines you follow daily, how you choose to live, and how helpful you are to others are the subject matter described by this house.

7th House-The House of Partnerships

The seventh house is ruled by the sign of Libra. This is your interaction and relationships with other people. These are the relationships that are both personal and business nature. This house outlines the contracts, business deals, and marriages that transpire.

8th House-The House of Reincarnation

The eighth house is ruled by the sign of Scorpio and offers a lot to the imagination. This house is a catch-all drawer for your life. It handles the mysteries, death, deep levels, birth, sex, and transformations in your life. This house also has dealings in the subject area of money on things like real estate and inheritances. Like I said, it's a catch-all.

9th House-The House of Philosophy

The ninth house of the zodiac wheel is ruled by the sign of Sagittarius. Covered in this house includes things like higher education, mind expansion, international and long-distance travel, learning foreign languages, optimism, risk, luck, religion, morals, ethics, and inspiration.

10th House-The House of Social Status

The tenth house of the zodiac wheel is ruled by the sign of Capricorn. This is the house that is at the very top of the wheel and also the house that is most public. On the cusp of this house, astrologers can tell you what your career path is and should be in life. This house is governing structures, tradition, corporations, public image, awards and achievements, discipline, and fame.

11th House-The House of Friendships

The eleventh house is ruled by the sign of Aquarius. This house rules the aspects of friendships in your life. It also influences teamwork, society, technology, networking, rebellions, social justices you stand for, and humanitarian causes that you find important. The promotion of individuality lies in this house as well. The ability to handle the eccentric, surprises, science fiction items, and all things futuristic can be found here.

12th House-The House of Undoing

The zodiac wheel is completed by the house that is ruled by the sign of Pisces. This final house is the one that brings things to an end. This covers things from finishing a project, the afterlife, how old age is going to go, and the ultimate surrender. It symbolizes the separation from society. It is also indicative of film, creativity, poetry, dance, the arts, journals, and all the things that occupy your subconscious mind.

Interpreting the Sections of a Birth Chart

The Zodiac Circle

The circle of the birth chart is divided into twelve sections. Each one of these sections is for the twelve signs of the zodiac. The innermost point of the circle, where all the divisions come together, is Earth (you). We know that the planets revolve around the Sun, but when trying to figure out the alignment of the planets to a given point in time, your birth, then you would have to center your focal point to Earth. Each of these sections is thirty degrees in size to equal the full three hundred and sixty degrees of the circle. This is an interpretation of the heavens split into twelve sectors.

The Circle of Houses

The next section comes in the form of the twelve houses represented by the birth signs. The way these are situated on the birth chart involves the exact time of your birth, that is why it is a critical piece of information. The first house is going to start with the moment of your birth and then work its way counterclockwise around the sections to depict the path of the Sun.

The Planets

Next, the planet placement will be placed on the birth chart. These planets will lay within the lined divisions you have made in the circle. Since the houses and the zodiac signs may not line up, it is imperative to place the planets exactly where they were at that exact moment. This is what gives a more accurate interpretation of your birth chart.

Rising Sign

Once the planets have been laid out, add the ascending, descending, medium Coeli, and immum Coeli axis lines. This will give a division between hemispheres on the chart. The rising sign is always going to be to the left of the division line. The rising sign is what your dominant sign is for a given attribute.

Lacking Elements on the Birth Chart

Your zodiac sign belongs to one of the four specific elements: Earth, Air, Fire, and Water. Each of these elements has its own special influence on the characteristics exhibited by each of these signs. In the same way, if your birth chart is lacking or missing an element, it can mean big things for you as well in terms of your personality traits.

Missing Fire

If you are missing Fire in your birth chart, it can make your personality seem pessimistic, apathetic, unmotivated, uninvolved, and unexcitable. This means, for lack of better terms, you are missing your spark. The flame that drives you is out or missing, and you have no drive or desire.

Missing Earth

Someone who is missing the element of Earth from their birth chart is often impractical, ungrounded, disorganized, unproductive, and impulsive. The Earth element is what keeps someone practical and firmly grounded with their roots in the soil of their birth. When lacking in the Earth element, it can feel like you have lost touch with yourself.

Missing Air

Air is the element that describes those who have a free spirit about them. If you are lacking or missing the air element, you will be unsociable, unaware of bias, uncommunicative, subjective, and inaccessible. These can hinder a person's ability to hold on to relationships with people. They are not able to socialize in a way that those are having the Air element present in their chart.

Missing Water

Water signs are full of emotion. The lack of or missing element of Water can cause someone to become somber, businesslike, closed off, controlling, and impersonal. Which is the complete opposite of the water character traits? This is a disservice to anyone who wants to be able to make connections in life, especially meaningful ones.

When you are missing an element, or lacking in it, an astrologer can give you ideas and recommendations to help equal out your life. The entire point of learning about your birth chart is to see what your strengths, weaknesses, and future outcomes look like. By using the chart as a foreshadowing tool, you can, in essence, head off problems before they arise.

Chapter 4: The Ascendant, Descendant, Midheaven, and Immum Coeli

The Ascendant, Descendant, Midheaven (Medium Coeli), and the Immum Coeli are known as the four angles on the birth chart. Planets that fall along, or are conjoined, at these points are important and have influence over a person's personality. These are also referred to as "angular planets."

To visualize, the Ascendant and the Descendant line are what divide the zodiac circle into upper and lower halves. The lower half of the circle symbolizes subjective experiences. The upper part of the circle symbolizes objectivity and your experiences with the outer world. The Midheaven and Immum Coeli lines divide the circle further into Eastern and Western halves. The Eastern half is about yourself, and the Western is how other's impact your life. Where the planets fall in these hemispheres is what shows the more prominent characteristics of a person.

The Ascendant and Descendant Axis

The ascendant is classified as a point that rises on the eastern horizon at a given moment (birth), and moves as the Earth rotates on its axis. The descendant is the same point, only on the western horizon, straight across from the ascendant point. To make it simpler, if you are in a dark room and you turn on a flashlight. The point in which the light hits the wall across from you would be like the descendant point and the origin (you) are the ascendant. This axis is what powers the power of attraction. The axis starts with the first house and goes to the seventh house. The ascendant is the point that draws in things like marriages and close relationships. The sign that falls under the ascendant are what describe your personality and how you react toward others. This is your "self" reaction to things. The ascendant is also known as the "rising sign." This is the sign that gives your outer appearance. This is the personality you wear on the outside.

The descendant is the opposite of that. It is the "them" of the axis. The sign it falls underon the descendant point is how you will interact with others. The sign under the descendant point is how we handle our interpersonal relationships. Close study of the descendant can often teach us why we tend to repeat the same acts over and over again.

The Midheaven (Medium Coeli) and Immum Coeli

The Medium Coeli is Latin for "middle of the sky." The immum Coeli is Latin for "bottom of the sky." This axis is what divides the circle into the eastern and western halves. This line is important because it defines the inner and outer self-projections of yourself. The Medium Coeli is our first point of outer-awareness on a birth chart. It represents our ego and interpretation of our environment from birth and on.

The immum Coeli is the first point of inner-awareness on a birth chart. This is also known as the "id." This is the personality we are born with, our roots. The sign under the immum Coeli is what describes the qualities that mold your id, while the sign under the medium Coeli is what molds the ego.

Zodiac Pairings on the Ascendant and Descendant Axis

The ascendant and the descendant axis make up the line that is synonymous with the power of attraction. What this means is that there is an attraction between two signs that are connected by this axis. It is a powerful attraction that is magnetic and is the Universes way of drawing them together. The law itself is responsible for bringing together those who have similar thoughts, situations, ideas, and circumstances.

Aries and Libra

The relationship between these two signs is what forms the path to learn about one's true identity. These two signs are from born in different parts of the year; however, they completely understand each other.

Taurus and Scorpio

These signs are driven by their creativity and their intense sexual energies. They are able to explore and experience life energy through each other.

Gemini and Sagittarius

These signs are driven by the sense of adventure and having someone to share it with. Their identity urges them to find others who they can find truth with and support relationships based on freedom and space to be themselves.

Cancer and Capricorn

Cancer and Capricorn signs are drawn by the idea of family. It may not mean the same to each other, but they are committed to the idea of stability and community within their own definition of family. This is why they work so well together.

Leo and Aquarius

These two signs complement each other. They are willing to explore relationships that allow them to experience freedom along with interdependency. These signs like to celebrate each other and their unique qualities but still maintain individual goals.

Virgo and Pisces

These are philanthropic signs. They believe that there is a higher work to be done. They prefer to build upon a committed relationship that is of a spiritual path and a devotion to a higher power.

Chapter 5: Numerology

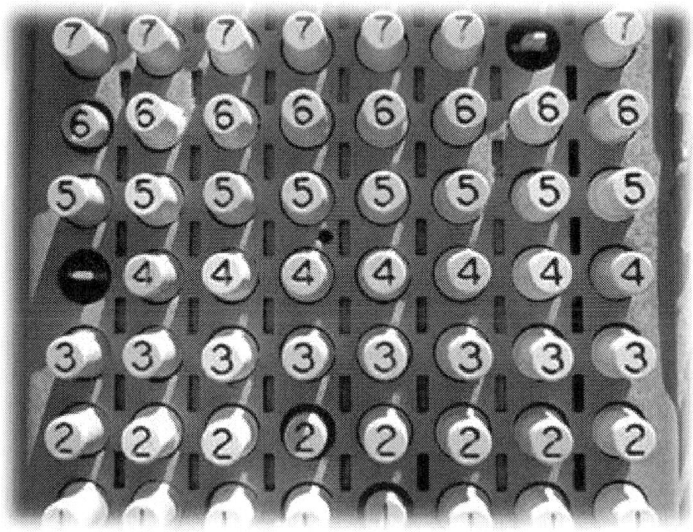

Numerology is the belief that there is a divine and mystical relationship between numbers and one or more events in your life. The earliest record is said to begin back in ancient Egypt and Babylon. Other evidence shows that a form of it was used several thousands of years ago in Rome, Greece, China, and Japan.

The use of numerology in the modern-day sense is credited to Pythagoras, the Greek philosopher. It is not known if he actually was the one who invented it, but he held multiple theories behind it. It was Dr. Julian Stenton in the early 1900's who came up with the name 'numerology.'

How Numerology Works

The actual science of Numerology is a complicated one. It requires a master numerologist to interpret the readings. Years of study are generally required to master the art.

As a novice, there are basic calculations that you can do to find your life path number, your expression number, your personality number, and your soul urge numbers. It is how the numbers function as a whole that you need to have an expert interpret if you are going past the basic principle.

The basic idea behind Numerology is that the cosmos and your life are affected by things like your birth date and your birth name. There are many other factors that play into this as well that surround you. A Numerology forecast can provide you with the various layers that these factors play in your life. This forecast is something that can provide a deep insight into your life.

There are no coincidences in the Universe, according to the philosophy of Numerology. There is only the fact that your name and birth date affect the journey you are supposed to embark on. This is the same way that horoscopes and astrology interpret the signs and destinies of the person it describes.

There are a lot of different calculations that occur in finding your Numerology numbers. These calculations can go into many depths and combinations regarding your life. Basic readings with basic core numbers can offer a lot of insight into your life, but since numbers are infinite, a numerology chart can continue to be read from different perspectives like a project that is ongoing.

Life Path Number

Your life path number is the most important number in your Numerology reading. It forms the foundation of the path that your life should take. It should reflect who you are as a person, at least who you were meant to be, in regard to your personality and traits. Life path numbers also outline opportunities or challenges that you may face in your life as well; it represents the lessons you may learn in your life along the way as well.

You calculate your life path number using your birth date. To show an example, say that your birth date is January 16, 1987. The goal is to reduce this down to a single digit by adding all of the numbers.

1+1+6+1+9+8+7=32

3+2=5

The life path number would be 5.

Life Path Number 1

The life path number of one means that you are dedicated, and you are creative. You are naturally inclined to follow through with the goals you set. Your law of attraction gifts center around visualization and the creation of dream boards. The use of dream boards for you is more powerful than verbal affirmations.

On the flip side of this number, you are on a constant journey to please people. This makes you ignore the things that you actually want in your life and rely too much on the opinions of others versus your needs and desires.

Life Path Number 2

The life path number of two is reserved for the people who are emotionally sensitive and are truly genuine. These people practice honestly as a general rule and try to tune out desires when decision making.

The flip side for this number is challenged by the constant feeling that they let people down, and they feel defeated and hopeless a lot of the time when these feelings hit them. Trying to keep a positive mindset can help this side from manifesting and taking control.

Life Path Number 3

The life path number three means that you are a social magnet. Anything that involves people is an easy thing. Networking and romance especially come easy to a number three. You have a large amount of optimism for the future for a good majority of the time.

The flip side of this number is that there is a lot of flippancy and commitment problems for this number. It is hard for a three to pinpoint one thing and devote time and energy to it.

Life Path Number 4

Life path number fours are blessed with a practical personality and a very strong will. This life number is the one who is most likely to believe in the law of attraction and what people take from it. You like to formulate plans before doing things.

On the flip side, the number four is more likely to miss out on spontaneous opportunities due to their structured nature. They are also less likely to end up wealthy.

Life Path Number 5

Those who are born with a life number of five are more likely to be open-minded and flexible thinkers. They are more likely to find solutions outside of the box when faced with a problem. They are into the present moment, and less likely to be bogged down by memories of the past and worries about their future.

The flip side of five is that they are rather self-indulgent. They are more into passing pleasures than investing in a change that could last for them. They are self-focused and tend to use their positivity to manifest it onto other people.

Life Path Number 6

The life path number six is the definition of a true Samaritan. This number is so compassionate and generous that they can't stop themselves from spreading goodness in every place they go. They are nurturing and are always full of energy that radiates love.

The other side of a six is that they are always spending too much time giving to others that they have trouble finding time to take care of themselves. This makes it to where a six always seems just to be outside of the grasp of reaching what they want for their life.

Life Path Number 7

A life path number of seven is a peaceful and reflective person. They know how to enjoy connecting with others, and they do not allow it to define who they are. Sevens are already in a mindset that gives them a balanced and satisfying relationship type.

The other side of seven is that they have trouble appreciating what they have sometimes. They are more skeptical about the things that they cannot prove.

Life Path Number 8

Those with a life path number of eight have a personality that is determined and focused but remain thoughtful about their surroundings. They are great organizers who are practical and confident.

The other side of this number means that they spend so much time being practical that they rarely give themselves the opportunity to dream, and they often struggle to find a true and long-lasting love.

Life Path Number 9

Life path numbers of nine generally receive automatic respect from people. This number makes a person honorable with a sense of fairness to them. The number nine has a charm that is charismatic, and other people find themselves drawn to a nine. Harnessing this magnetism, a nine radiates can help them attract all the things that they desire in life.

The other side of the nine gets in the way a lot. They spend a lot of time being negative and obsessive about having the perfect life. These negative thoughts often stop them from achieving them.

Expression Number

The expression number is also known as your destiny number. It is said to expose your abilities, personal goals, and desires. It is also able to make you aware of the traits that you may inherently carry.

Your expression number is compiled by using your entire birth name. First, middle and last names are converted into numbers using the Pythagorean Numerology Chart. This chart assigns a numerical single-digit value to a single letter. You then add up the total down to one number, much like the life path number.

1	2	3	4	5	6	7	8	9
A	B	C	D	E	F	G	H	I
J	K	L	M	N	O	P	Q	R
S	T	U	V	W	X	Y	Z	

Expression Number 1

An expression number of one means that a person is a natural-born leader with a lot of courage, ambition, and influence. Because of the perfectionist tendencies, it is important to remember not to undermine yourself, especially in relationships.

Expression Number 2

An expression number of two means that a person is friendly and intuitive. They have a sensitive soul and are great at working alongside others. The downside to being a two is that your feelings end up hurt easily because of your willingness to be open and your lack of personal boundaries.

Expression Number 3

An expression number of three means that a person generally is an inspiration to those around them. They are highly energetic and expressive. They can lift the moods of people around them and tend to do a good job thriving in any situation. The creativity side to you makes it hard to commit to any one task, and you are constantly changing them.

Expression Number 4

An expression number of four means that a person has a great eye for detail and is usually very methodical in their thinking. You are extremely stubborn, which in the wrong circumstances, can cause problems for you. Use your good problem-solving skills instead of your stubbornness.

Expression Number 5

An expression number of five is reserved for the person who loves the thrill of adventure. These are the people who love exciting things and the diversity that they bring. They have excellent communication skills, and with a little work on their own self-discipline, they can achieve anything they put their minds to.

Expression Number 6

An expression number of six is the most loving and devoted of the expression numbers. They are caring and nurturing of others in relationships, which gives them the tendency to ignore their own needs. A number six needs to remember to use the responsible side of their traits to avoid that from happening.

Expression Number 7

An expression number of seven brings the thirst for knowledge. Sevens have a gift for analyzing information and are generally found in scientific or technological career fields. They can be an introvert, so it is important for a seven to remember that other people can offer them just as much fulfillment.

Expression Number 8

An expression number of eight is a highly competitive personality. They are deeply determined to get things done and can be distracted by a materialistic lifestyle at first, but once they get past that, they begin to see what a spiritual awakening can do for them and their abilities.

Expression Number 9

An expression number of nine describes an idealistic person who is motivated by giving everyone a fair chance and seeing the good that people possess. There is a large amount of underlying self-doubt inside of a nine, but it is important for them to realize that other people are not as critical of them as they are of themselves.

Soul Urge Number

The soul urge number is also known as the "heart's desire" number. This number is derived from your birth name, but only the vowels in it. This is the number that represents your inner self, and it knows what motivates you. This number is also capable of showing you the reasons behind some of the decisions that you make.

Since it is derived from the vowels in your name, it is important to know when "y" is a vowel. If your name has a "y" in it that has the sound of "e," then it is considered a vowel. The vowels in your name are then assigned a specific number. They are added together like the expression number until you have reduced to a single digit.

A	E	I	O	U	Y
1	5	9	6	3	7

Soul Urge/Heart's Desire Number 1

A soul urge/heart's desire number of one are natural-born leaders. These people are ones who are independent and can take care of themselves well. They have a clear mind, and they have a clear vision of their goals and purpose in life.

These people are obsessed with their own ideas, and it is often hard to convince them otherwise. They are extremely protective of the ones they love and demand respect from other people.

Soul Urge/Heart's Desire Number 2

A soul urge/heart's desire of two is caring, artistic, and loving. These people have very calm natures, peaceful, and well mannered. These people have a large imagination, which allows them to be creative.

Twos like to test out their ideas instead of allowing themselves to be spontaneous with their creative abilities. The best describing factors of the soul urge of two is their positive energy, companionship, balance, and ability to work as a team.

Soul Urge/Heart's Desire Number 3

A soul urge/heart's desire three is the strongest number in numerology. If you possess this number, then you are a strong individual who remains focused and determined.

You reach your goals by using your optimistic outlook, bravery, enthusiasm, and compassion.

The greatest satisfaction in your life comes from your desire and ability to accomplish anything. This pleases you because you will be remembered for years to come. You are focused and constantly thinking about your future.

Soul Urge/Heart's Desire Number 4

A soul urge/heart's desire four is one who likes structure in their lives. They require stability and always have plans for getting things done. Those who are number fours are considered to be well mannered, stable, and well organized. This is the number of persistence.

Fours have trouble accepting when things do not go according to plan. They do not accept change very well in that way. They become frustrated when they are not able to control situations or plan for them in advance. This is why a four will continue to work on organizing and planning to perfect it.

Soul Urge/Heart's Desire Number 5

A soul urge/heart's desire five yearns for freedom. This number likes to travel and have new experiences, which includes meeting new people as well. The number five is brave and enthusiastic, which is why people see them as natural-born leaders.

The number five may be a natural-born leader, but they are full of a lot of self-doubt. This is due to their free spirit. They would rather be doing new and exciting things than be in charge of others.

Soul Urge/Heart's Desire Number 6

A soul urge/heart's desire six is full of love. They care deeply for other people and often take care of others before themselves. The number six is well-balanced, always true to what matters most, and full of harmony.

The number six is easily taken advantage of, though because they love so deeply. They think that by loving the way that they want to be loved, it will be returned, which is not always the case.

Soul Urge/Heart's Desire Number 7

A soul urge/heart's desire number seven is one that likes to avoid distractions and reflect on their own thoughts. For this reason, you will generally see a number seven as being shut off from the world. The mind of a seven is constantly analyzing everything around them, which is why they like to be alone and shut that part of them off when they can.

Sevens are ambitious individuals and come across as not caring what is going on with others around them, but that is because they are too busy with everything thing else their heads are filled with. This number is a big dreamer and is often full of unique opinions on things.

Soul Urge/Heart's Desire Number 8

A soul urge/heart's desire number eight has the confidence inside them, unlike any other number. This confidence, in conjunction with their ambition, allows them to become and achieve anything that they set out to do in life. Eights do aspire to be rich and possess material items, but they have the built-in capability to do so.

The number eight is good at organizing, and they prefer to be the ones to keep things running smoothly. They are able to make decisions quick and effective in situations that call for them. Their sharp minds make business an ideal job for the number 8.

Soul Urge/Heart's Desire Number 9

A soul urge/heart's desire number nine is the biggest dreamer, and the most selfless number among those of the soul urge numbers. These people are extremely sympathetic and charismatic. They want to make the world a better place for themselves and everyone around them.

Nines can be a little emotionally unstable, though. They tend to get upset quickly. They prefer to bring peace and harmony to the world so when conflicts arise between people, they can become quite sad. It is important though for a nine to figure out how to deal with these feelings.

Personality Number

The personality number in the world of Numerology is the one that explains the characteristics, qualities, traits, and tendencies that you are sending out into the Universe. This number tells what kinds of people you like and why your personality is the way it is.

Figuring out your personality number is much like the soul urge number, only with the consonants. Using the chart below, you find the numbers then add them until they are a single digit.

1	2	3	4	5	6	7	8	9
J	B	C	D	N	F	G	H	R
S	K	L	M	W	X	P	Q	
	T		V			Y	Z	

Personality Number 1

The personality number one describes a person who is classified as a natural-born leader. These people are ambitious and self-driven in life. These people are pioneers at work but will often soften their tone so that people who are less confident can get closer to them.

Personality Number 2

The personality number two describes a person who is a very reliable friend. They are honest and trustworthy. The number two is full of ideas and has many talents. They are often admired for their gentle and warm appearance but do not be fooled because they will push back their shyness if they need to fight for the things that they believe in.

Personality Number 3

The personality number three describes the people who seem to be intelligent, opportunistic, and lucky. They know how to tap into their intuitive properties, and they have excellent communicative skills, which attract people. They come across as manipulative, but this is because they are talkative, and their good decisions make them successful.

Personality Number 4

The personality number four describes the people who find family at the center of their world. They are genuine and are generally well-dressed. They prefer for everything around them to be in order, down to the finest detail. The number four comes across as boring in nature, but their stability and nurturing nature often come through.

Personality Number 5

The personality number five describes the people who are high spirited and like to be free. These people tend to travel a lot and can adapt to any situation that they may find themselves in. They are the first to take on challenges and take risks. They handle these situations with ease. They do like to overburden themselves with work, so it is good for them to find a medium place.

Personality Number 6

The personality number six describes the people who are typically described as warm and well-balanced in nature. They were born with a heart of gold and preferred to work on the inner self versus the outer appearance. The number six is friendly and likes to take care of the people that they meet.

Personality Number 7

The personality number seven describes the people who tend to be scholars by nature. They are intelligent and take a rational approach toward their situations. They are mysterious, but they radiate dignity and quality. They are also excellent poets and you may find them weird. They have an "I don't care" attitude about it though.

Personality Number 8

The personality number eight describes people who are born with the amazing ability to make judgments. They are highly successful people who may be less popular with people because they like to flaunt their success with materialistic items. The number eight is strong and can dominate in any situation. These people are extremely persuasive as well.

Personality Number 9

The personality number nine describes people who are natural-born philanthropists. These are the people who come across as arrogant, but after meeting them, you find out that they are truly charming and are full of confidence and influential.

Birth Date Number

Your birth date number in Numerology is literally just that, your birth date. The number of the month (1-31) on which you were born. Each one of these numbers holds a different trait that can give you more insight into yourself.

1st

If you were born on the first of the month, you are a natural-born leader. You have a determined will who gains the support of others easily. You are highly independent and would rather work alone, and not with the help of others.

2nd

If you were born on the second of the month, you were born with a warm demeanor that comes in handy when mediating for others. You are sensitive yet still maintain a level of diplomacy when dealing with those around you.

3rd

If you were born on the third of the month, you are a natural-born artist and contain a highly creative natural talent. You are a social star due to your affectionate wit and demeanor.

4th

If you were born on the fourth of the month, you are the dream of every employer. You are hard-working and detail-oriented with the ability to maintain a high compassion for those around you, especially family.

5th

If you were born on the fifth of the month, you are full of wanderlust. You like to travel and have a deep-seated desire to be free. You are a person who can adapt to any situation and you are extremely communicative which makes it easy for you to talk to others.

6th

If you were born on the sixth of the month, you are a generous family-oriented person. You possess a kind soul and are highly talented at keeping the peace in situations. You are the one to go to when looking to find the middle ground in a family squabble.

7th

If you were born on the seventh of the month, you are very mind oriented. You have a great sense of focus and a high level of intuition. You do not accept anything at face value and prefer to contemplate and explore all the topics you can. You typically are able to find the truth when others cannot.

8th

If you were born on the eighth of the month, you are a dreamer. You have the ability to take a creative approach when it comes to your money and business ventures because of your ability to dream up new ventures. You are always up for a challenge because you are efficient, confident with your skills, and realistic.

9th

If you were born on the ninth of the month, you are a true humanitarian. You carry with you an open mind and compassion for those around you. You are a charming person and find it easy to relate to others, no matter what your differences to them may be.

10th

If you were born on the tenth of the month, you are highly ambitious, and you want independence. You want to follow your own dreams in any way that you see fit. You are driven by a strong sense of success which allows you to rely on your strong analytical mind and your strong managerial skills.

11th

If you were born on the eleventh of the month, you have the mind of an optimist but understand enough that you are not naïve. Your dreamy mind is matched by your ability to be confident and determined. Your intuitive nature allows you to reach understandings with others.

12th

If you were born on the twelfth of the month, you have a natural artistic nature. You incorporate creativity in everything from your home to your daily life. You like to express yourself. You are more than likely the brightest light in your group of friends.

13th

If you were born on the thirteenth of the month, you are the most dependable in your family and community. You are a very organized and detail-oriented person who uses those abilities from work to artistic ventures.

14th

If you were born on the fourteenth of the month, you are one with a restless nature. You tend to gravitate toward the unexpected twists and turns that life throws at you, but you do possess a very analytical mind which makes you able to communicate and be social.

15th

If you were born on the fifteenth of the month, you are full of artistic talent. You are full of strong instincts in regard to business and finances, but your sensitivity allows others to feel like you are accessible to them.

16th

If you were born on the sixteenth of the month, you never feel like you are at home in the real world. You love to concentrate on big ideas. You have a great intuition which is why your interests seem to be focused on the spiritual and philosophical realms of life.

17th

If you were born on the seventeenth of the month, you are balanced by your ambitions and your skills with finances and business. You use practical judgment which is motivational to everyone you meet.

18th

If you were born on the eighteenth of the month, you are another natural-born leader, but your abilities also inspire the people around you. You possess an amazing understanding of people which makes you an ideal manager or politician. You have a broad mind and can express your feelings well.

19th

If you were born on the nineteenth of the month, you are ambitious but thrive on your independence. The risk-taking nature you have is balanced out by your creativity. This, combined with your sensitivity, helps you succeed with everything you face along your path.

20th

If you were born on the twentieth of the month, you are a walking mood ring. You wear your feelings, worries, and fears on the outside and everyone knows them. You are full of sensitivity and you are strong, but you have to make sure to keep a healthy distance from those around you.

21st

If you were born on the twenty-first of the month, you are full of unique visions and creative ideas that are fueled by your desire to be successful. You have a passionate nature, and this is reflected in the way you love others.

22nd

If you were born on the twenty-second of the month, you have a strong professional drive. You tend to be more innovative in business ventures and aren't a fan of supporting the status quo. You are capable of visualizing what you want and making it happen, all at the same time.

23rd

If you were born on the twenty-third of the month, you are adaptable and considered easy to get along with. You love when things change and are excited by the risk. You have strong skills in the love and communication department, but your versatile mind loves the experience something new brings to it.

24th

If you were born on the twenty-fourth of the month, you are extremely family-oriented. You possess an emotional soul that is willing to sacrifice for others which helps you bring peace and balance to the situations that may arise around you. You are good at bringing harmony to your relationships and your largest skills are healing and meditation.

25th

If you were born on the twenty-fifth of the month, you have the gift of broad knowledge and understanding which makes you the one to make decisions wisely. You are balanced and strong, full of intuition.

26th

If you were born on the twenty-sixth of the month, you possess a daring mindset that partners great with your strong sense of business and finances. You are a confident and capable leader as long as you don't lose sight of the bigger picture.

27th

If you were born on the twenty-seventh of the month, you have the natural ability to be a manager and lead people by inspiring them. You have a strong sense of organization. You also have the ability to be creative which makes you a double threat and ideally suited for careers such as art, politics, and law.

28th

If you were born on the twenty-eighth of the month, you like to be a leader, but only if there is a good sense of teamwork and cooperation between everyone involved. You may come across as having a rational mind, but underneath you operate with unconventional and idealistic thoughts.

29th

If you were born on the twenty-ninth of the month, you were born with a great imagination. You prefer to take a visual approach when it comes to your life. You prefer to use your intuition abilities to connect to a higher spiritual force.

30th

If you were born on the thirtieth of the month, you are the true definition of an artist. You are a social person and others see you as charming. You try to find a sense of harmony in everything that you do. You have to work hard to keep a balance between your imagination and discipline in daily life.

31st

If you were born on the thirty-first of the month, you would honor tradition and family. You prefer to make a solid foundation among the ones you love, and you tend to draw support and appreciation from others because of your natural tendency to be drawn to detail. You are always drawn to make the most out of the opportunities that come your way.

The Affects Numerology Has on Your Life

You have taken the journey of finding out how Numerology and specific numbers impact you as a person. Numerology doesn't just affect you, though, it also affects the things in your life as well. It has an influence on what paths or choices you may make in regard to life, career, and love.

Influence on Life Path

Your life path is the essence of your life. Every challenge, opportunity, and lesson during the span of your life is related to the Numerology behind the life path number. If you want to know where your life is essentially going to go and what you are going to face, your reading with your life path number can tell you.

Influence on Your Personality

Your personality is the DNA of who you are. The personality number that Numerology uncovers about us it the core of who we are as a person. Every action we take, every situation we face, and how we handle it, are all aspects of our personality. Numerology readings regarding your personality show you exactly who you are as a person, and no matter how we try to fight it, our personality is something we were born with and it is impossible to deny it.

Influence on Career

Choosing a career path is influenced directly and indirectly by our Numerology. We are people who are composed of so many different traits that once our reading is complete, it can show us where we were naturally born to rule. Think of it in terms of those tests that we were all made to take in high school. The ones that supposedly shows you what profession you are supposedly made for. Your Numerology numbers do something like this but consider your total person, not just who you are on the surface.

Influence on Our Interests

Because we are all composed of different traits, we are naturally made to enjoy certain things while detesting others. If you have a Numerology reading that shows you like to spend time on your own surrounded by books, it is highly unlikely that you are going to want to drop everything and travel the world on a whim. This works the same vice versa. When we know who we are and who we are meant to be based on our numerological makeup, it is easier to accept and explain the things that other people may find abnormal in our lives.

Influence on Attitude

The first thing that people tend to notice about another person is their attitude. There is a good chance that the way you come across to other people can be explained in greater detail based on your numerology reading. We are all composed of different numbers and paths, which can have a severe influence on our attitudes. Someone may interpret an attitude that is strong-willed as being defiant when in reality, you are simply focused on your goals.

Influence on Relationships and Compatibility

Besides the incompatibility that you learned with the Zodiac, there are also incompatibilities that occur with the Numerology numbers as well. There are a lot of things that are required to make a relationship with someone else work, and sometimes what happens is that we are simply just not compatible. Personalities can clash just like the courses we want to take with our lives can clash. It would not be any one person's fault if the incompatibility was naturally destined to happen due to the incompatibility of Numerology readings.

Influence on Location

It is proven that every city and state have their own numerological vibration, which means that if you have ever felt out of place somewhere, chances are you were not compatible with the numbers. Before changing your scenery, it might be worth talking to an expert numerologist to find out about the vibrations of the place you are thinking of moving. Much like relationships, it is not your fault for feeling averse to a place. You are just not numerically wired to belong there.

Influence on a Home

Just like the vibrations, a location can possess, the same can apply to your new address. Your home or apartment can have its own numerical vibrations, and if you are not compatible with it, you may never feel at home. It might be worth your time to get a Numerology reading for your potential home just to make sure that you are compatibly going to be comfortable.

Influence on Pets

Your pet is a person too, so in the same way that you have numerical vibes, so does your pet. The name you choose can have a huge influence on their personality, thanks to the vibrations from the name and the astrological values predestined for them. You can find out your pet's reading by using the same Numerology calculations done on your own name.

Influence on Business Ventures

The name of your business can be converted into a numerological reading as well. Just like you and your pet, the path that your business name falls under will be an indicator of the success or wealth it may attain. If you and your business's life path numbers are compatible, it can prove to be extremely prosperous for you.

Chapter 6: Kundalini Rising

Kundalini is rooted in the Hindu religion and is said to be a religious experience that is a kind of cosmic energy that radiates from the base of the spine. When awakened, it is said that the Kundalini can be felt from the base of the spine all the way through the top of the head. It is believed that the Kundalini rising is achieved through various chakras and when it does, you are to have achieved different levels of awakening.

History of Kundalini

The exact origin of Kundalini is not known for certain other than it was mentioned in a sacred Vedic collection of writings known as the Upanishads. The historical records point to Kundalini as a science of energy and spiritual philosophy prior to the physical practice being developed. The word "Upanishads" is translated to "sitting down to listen to the master's teachings."

In the beginning, Kundalini yoga was not taught publicly. It was considered an advanced education course taught by the masters to their students. Students were required to go through many years of training before being allowed to learn the way of Kundalini.

The actual science of Kundalini was kept secret for thousands of years. The secret was kept by one master who passed it down to a pupil of his choosing whom he felt was worthy to carry on the tradition. That was until one day when Yogi Bhajan came to Canada in 1968.

Yogi Bhajan was visiting the state of California toward the end of the 1960s when he came across the hippie revolution and identified two issues with their search for more. He noticed that all of them were looking for a way to be closer to God and that in their efforts to do so, they relied on drugs. He knew that teaching Kundalini was against sacred tradition; he had a vision during meditation that would awaken a new spirituality that combined his knowledge and modern practicalities. It is this that made Yogi Bhajan responsible for the Kundalini movement that took the Western hemisphere.

Kundalini Yoga

Kundalini yoga is one of the oldest yogi arts that deal with the transformation in addition to the expanding of consciousness. The emergence of the Kundalini energy going up the spine and through the chakras, which are the energy centers of the body, and helps with activating and balancing the chakras by uniting the cosmic energy with the energies that hold down the Kundalini. Using breathing exercises, body locks, exercise sets, postures, gestures, and sounds, the Kundalini can rise and be awakened.

By using the practice of Kundalini yoga, the student can unite their consciousness with the cosmic consciousness around them by performing the exercises and meditations in a specific order and combination on a regular basis, thus making it more efficient. The student will soon be able to feel the energy not only within them but around them as well and will be able to consciously awaken their chakras.

Kundalini Yoga Poses

Kundalini yoga poses are also called asanas. Asanas generally apply pressure on your nerves and acupressure points in your body, which reflexes to the brain and body to allow for certain effects. These poses are generally to help with stimulating the organs and glands for better body awareness.

(Sukhasana) Easy Pose

To perform the easy pose, cross feet allowing your ankles to touch, or place both feet flat on the floor. Press your bottom most point of your spine up and keep your back straight.

(Siddhasana) Perfect Pose

Start with sukasana and at the perineum, press into it with the heel on your right foot, the sole of your foot should be resting on the left upper thigh. Place the heel of your left foot over the top of the right foot so that you are pressing upward with your toes tucked between the thigh and calf muscle. Your knees should be resting on the ground with your heels directly above one another.

This is the most comfortable asana position and is considered to be the one to promote the most psychic power.

(Padmasana) Lotus Pose

Starting with the easy pose, lift your left foot up and onto the upper part of the thigh on your right leg. Then your left foot should be resting on the upper part of your left thigh. Make sure to keep them near your body as possible. This is a safe posture that is simpler than it sounds, and it is a good way to enhance deep meditative states. Make sure that you always have your right leg on top.

(Vajrasana) Rock Pose

Kneel, sitting on the back of your heels. The top of your feet should be flat on the floor. Make sure that the heels are pressing into the nerves that are positioned in the middle of your rear end. They called this the rock pose because of its help in the digestive process.

Hero (Celibate) Pose

Along with your feet positioned equidistant to your hips, go down on your knees and sit in sandwiched between your feet. Hero (celibate) pose helps channel sensual power up the spinal column.

Deep Breathing Techniques (Pranayama)

For practitioners of Kundalini that have been doing the deep breathing techniques for many years, it is a natural thing that occurs for them. A lot of the time, a newer student will fill the lower abdomen area of the lungs and then try to fill the chest area but do not keep the right pressure, and the complete breath is only obtained in the chest cavity. This is not the diaphragm breathing that is needed.

Long Deep Breathing

Long deep breathing is a good way to relax and is often the first breathing technique that is taught when starting Kundalini. This also helps those who have lung-related issues with building up their lung capacity.

You begin by sitting with your legs crossed. You then take in a deep breath filling the abdominal area by pushing the air downward, then pressing the air into the lower areas. By arching your body somewhat forward and resting your palms on your knees, your chest cavity can begin to open forward. This allows you to keep pressure on the lungs and the abdominal area.

Once your lungs have been completely filled, hold the breath for a moment while pushing your shoulders back to expand the chest outward. You should feel the full pressure of the diaphragm at this point. Once you feel this, contract your diaphragm and push out the air.

The purpose of breathing this way through the nose for several of these breaths is to help the flow of energy and consciousness. This also helps with the blood circulation because of the involvement of the lungs and the deep breaths that circulate through them.

The pressure that is generated when the lungs are full and then contracted helps generate energy that stimulates the nerve endings. This helps engage the entire body in the process.

Once this type of deep breathing has been accomplished several times, you will find that it becomes a lot more natural. You will also begin to feel the motion that the entire diaphragm is involved during the whole breathing cycle.

Breath of Fire (Agni-Prasana)

The breath of fire is an energizing breath that is cleansing to the body, and that is powered through spasms of the abdomen.

Once the long deep breathing technique has been mastered and you can feel the diaphragm, then you can begin the breath of fire technique. This begins with the long deep breathing technique. Once you take the air in, you do not hold; you immediately let it out. Once it has been let out, you immediately bring in another breath. You keep doing this process. It is reminiscent of a locomotive engine lurching on the tracks.

With each breath, you replace it with another until a nice rhythm begins to form out of the breathing. The breath of fire is meant to help charge the nervous system. It allows your glands to secrete the hormones you need and the blood to purify. Using this breathing technique for periods of time can help strengthen the mind and allows the body to become more connected to the mind.

Mantras and Kundalini

The universe is made up of different frequencies of sound. All of these frequencies are energy, and all energy send out vibrations. Mantras are the way that the Universe speaks to us. These frequencies are used like a tuning fork and helps harness particular universal frequencies.

When a particular sound is being chanted, the energy field around our body reflects that. We make a connection with the frequency that we are searching for by harnessing it in. A lot of what gravitates toward us is put out there by our own minds, even if we do not realize it. Chants are the device that we can use to deprogram that auto-tune that we put on our minds. The mantras that we use can help us open the channels of our mind to be receptive to the energy we are searching for.

Meditation and Kundalini

Meditation is not magical, nor is it a religion to be believed among the masses. It is an established practice that is used to create a means of communication among your conscious and subconscious mind. Think of meditation as your own personal "me time." You connect with your breath, your mind, your body, and your soul. You allow thoughts to escape your mind and truly find peace with just being.

By using meditation as a daily ritual, you can help keep your mind clean of the clutter that we can all build up in our lives. You are in charge of this time with you. It cannot be undone by someone else. You use this time with yourself, like you would use your time in the shower. You clean your mind of the things that bog it down and make it feel dirty.

Use the time you meditate to keep a calmness around you and to escape from the hustle and bustle of everyday life. By allowing yourself to have time to meditate, you can rejuvenate your mind and help recharge your body. The use of meditation can help handle the stress that may stop your body from unleashing its full energy potential.

When and Where to Meditate

Find a place where you cannot be disturbed. Make sure that the temperature in that area is comfortable. Find a seat on something that is comfortable and cushioned. Those who practice the art of Kundalini yoga prefer to use thick wool or sheepskin blankets for support. The whole point when meditating is to keep your spine as straight as possible because the spine is the center of your nervous system. A lot of meditation practitioners like to reserve a space in their home that is comfortable and used only for the sole purpose of meditation.

There is no set rule on time to practice meditation. A lot of people who are experienced with meditation like to practice in the early hours of the morning between four and eight because they are considered the ambrosial hours. Since nothing typically goes on during those times, it is easy to cut out the distractions from daily life. Some peoplc prefer to meditate in the evening before bed. This is so that they can open their minds and be in a more relaxed state before going to sleep. There is a larger chance that it will induce a deeper sleep if meditating prior to bedtime.

It is recommended not to meditate after eating due to the heaviness it creates in your stomach. It can make it uncomfortable and hard to focus and restricts the capacity of your brain from being receptive to the full benefits.

How Long to Meditate

The length of time a person meditates is dependent on them and their skill level at doing so. When starting out, it is hard to completely clear the mind and allow for relaxation, so starting out small can help a person learn the proper way to meditate.

Since this is a time for you to spend with only yourself, finding the right time and the amount of time is up to you. There is no general rule on how much time you will need to reach a full meditative state, but it is okay for you to work on building up your time so that you can reap the full benefits.

How to Meditate

Before trying to commit to one meditation style, try learning the basics of meditation first. Sound and breathing.

A lot of meditations incorporate the use of mantras. Sometimes these are simply words that are repeated that represent big thoughts you may have or a goal you want to meet. Using basic sounds or rhythms can help penetrate the conscious and redirect the movement of thinking, which makes room for other thoughts to enter.

Even though the words of a mantra may not make full sense to you, it isn't about the words necessarily but the energy behind the chant. It is about the hormone release that it unleashes in mind. There is a part of your mind that becomes more engaged when you are chanting, even if you don't fully understand the language or concept of it.

A lot of practitioners use mantras in their lives every day. Meditating causes an alteration of the brain patterns and chemistry, as well as emotional balance. Using a mantra at the same time can help reinforce these changes in the brain that are being facilitated.

There are three ways to use a mantra, and sometimes a meditation can use all three of them. The first is a regular or boisterous expression that is interpreted as being the normal language of all living things. The second one is a sharp mutter which is considered the voices used by lovers. The third is a chant that is silent or mentally driven which is the language of the divine and infinity.

There are two things that you can do for yourself to make the mantras stronger, regardless of how they are delivered. You can envision the mantra in your mind as if you were writing it on a piece of paper in your mind.

The other is to actively listen to the mantra and take it in fully.

Pranayam (Breath)

A lot of meditations revolve around the idea of focused breathing. Just listen to your flow of breath or the pattern in which you are breathing; you can help push out the thoughts that are overwhelming your mind. The breath is correlated to your mood and your energy levels, this means that altering your breath patterns can affect your mood and energy levels as well.

Make sure that when you are using breathing exercises with your meditation that you are using a guide or an instructor. You need to make sure that you are following all of the recommendations as well as doing it as specified. You do not want to end up changing your breath in too extreme of a manner and ending up dizzy or lightheaded.

Mudras (Gestures)

A gesture, which is referred to as a mudra in Kundalini yoga, is usually made with the hands in an effort to lock energy flow and guide it. It is important to remember when practicing a mudra, to only exert enough pressure to help conductively flow the energy, but not enough to whiten the tips of the fingers.

Guyan Mudra

The guyan mudra is when you take your thumb and touch it to the index finger of the same hand. This is used to stimulate your knowledge and ability. The symbolic value of the pointer finger is the planet Jupiter, but the thumb is the ego. The point of this gesture is for receptivity and calm.

Active Guyan Mudra

The active guyan mudra is when you take the first bend in the pointer finger and bend it under the first bend in your thumb on the same hand. This is to impart active knowledge.

Shuni Mudra

The shuni mudra is when you take the tip of your middle finger, which is symbolic of the planet Saturn, and touch the tip of the thumb. This is to give yourself patience.

Surya or Ravi Mudra

The surya or ravi mudra is when you take your ring finger, which symbolizes the Sun or Uranus cosmically and touch it to the tip of your thumb to give yourself health, energy, and intuition.

Buddhi Mudra

The buddhi mudra is when you take the tip of your little finger, which is symbolic of Mercury, and touch it to the tip of your thumb to help yourself with clear and intuitive communication.

Venus Lock

To complete the Venus lock, interlace your fingers with the pinky finger on your left hand at the bottom most point. The right pointer should be positioned on top for men. The left pointer should be positioned on top for women. The heaps at the bottom most point of your thumb, which are referred to as Venus mounds, are pushed simultaneously to channel sensual and sexual feelings. The balance of the glands helps with concentrating and focusing.

Jupiter Mudra

To execute this Jupiter mudra, place both index fingers together like a gun. This is the invocation of Jupiter, which brings good luck when the expansion is activated. Together these can focus your energy and let it break through all the walls that are in its way.

Prayer Mudra

To do the prayer mudra, place the palms of your hands together as if you were praying. This is a neutralizing mudra that represents the yin and the yang and allows for you to center yourself.

Bear Grip

To complete the bear grip, you need to place your left hand facing outward in front of your body with your thumb facing down. Place your right hand in front of your body facing inward with your thumb up. Curl your fingers and hook them together. Exerting just enough energy can help accelerate your heart and bring better focus to your concentration.

Buddha Mudra

Hand placement is important for this one. The man will put the back of his left hand into his right palm. The woman will put the back of her right hand into her left palm. Make sure both of the palms are facing upward with your thumbs touching. The gesture is a receptive one.

Importance of Spinal Flexibility

People who teach Kundalini yoga say that age can be defined by the flexibility of one's spine. Ideally, the whole practice of Kundalini is to guard the spinal column because it is the center of your nervous system and the path in which the awakening will travel. Exercising your spine regularly can help you activate and align it to help with your reception of energies.

Lower back pain and stress on the upper back is a common complaint among most grown adults. By using exercises regularly, you can avoid the pains associated with chronic back issues. While there are no quick fixes, Kundalini can offer up a great maintenance program to help.

- To begin, sit, and quietly focus on your breathing. Make sure to slow down and think only about breathing from the belly. Allow yourself to feel the sensations in your body as they come. Tune into the rhythms that your body is telling you. Allow yourself to do this for a few minutes and allow your body to become calm. Feel yourself in your own safe and quiet space.
- Take a moment to make sure that you are tuning into yourself. Meditate and repeat the mantra "adi mantra" to fully tune yourself into the energy around you.
- Convert to the easy pose and place your hands onto your knees. Make sure to intensely turn your pelvic bone, swirling it in a rounded motion. Take

comfort in this movement and make it a meditation of movement for your entire body. Complete twenty-six revolutions for sixty to one-hundred and twenty seconds in each direction. The movement helps open the energy receptors in your back and helps by giving the organs a small massage to aid in the digestive process.

- While you are still seated in the easy pose, grab ahold of your ankles. As you inhale, flex your spinal column forward. Make sure you are keeping your shoulders relaxed and your head straight while doing this. Make sure that you are not moving your head in an up and down pattern. As you exhale the breath, relax, and return the spine to regular position. Resume with these rhythmic deep breaths. As you are inhaling, pay attention to the energy going down your spine. As you exhale the breath, feel it come back up and linger at the third eye chakra point. Mentally bring the feeling up and down the spine as you repeat. Do this for one to three minutes or up to one hundred and eight times. To end this part of the exercise, bring in a deep breath and hold. Exhale and relax. Sit quietly for a little while and feel the energy as it circulates through your body from your spine.

Spinal Flex on Heels

To execute the exercise on sitting on your heels, place your hands limply on top of the corresponding thigh. Resume the above flex exercise above with robust breathing. Repeat this for one to two minutes. This exercise loosens the spine toward the middle section and allows for the chakra of the heart to be opened.

Neck Rolls

Sitting position, allowing your spine to be straight, yet in a relaxed state. Allow your head to simply sit as if it were on a shelf, the shelf being the spinal column. Do this by slightly adjusting your head backwards with your chin pointed down. Roll your neck slowly and fluidly and rolling it one way and then in the other direction. Allow the weight of your head sitting atop your spine; do the movement for you. Make sure you are doing this in a methodical manner so that it is working those tight spots and loosening up the tension you hold in your neck. Do this for at least one minute in each direction for the full effect. At the end of the time, make sure to sit quietly and reflect on it. Feeling the energy and the sensations that are flowing through your body. This helps remove the tension held by the muscles of your neck and helps in stimulating the thyroid gland.

Side Twists

While sitting on your feet, bring your hands up to rest upon your shoulders. Your fingers should be resting by your neck facing the front of your body, and the thumbs should be lightly touching shoulder blades. Take in a deep breath and twist your body at the waist to the left. Exhale the breath while twisting your body at the waist to the right. Make sure that you are twisting your head as well. Your spine may feel tight when you first start, but as you continue to twist, you will feel your spine start to loosen up. Keep your elbows positioned at an equidistant space from the ground and allow your arms to move as they wish when you move your body. You can stand or sit to execute this exercise if sitting on your feet is too complicated. Go on twisting your body for one to two minutes or until you have completed the twist twenty-six times. At the end of the twists, take a breath and hold it. Exhale and relax your body allowing yourself to give in to the feeling of the energy.

Side Bends

Sitting in the basic pose (easy pose), fasten both of your hands at the back of your head in a locked Venus position. Keep your fingers intertwined. Bending your body straight down your side, aim your elbow to the floor and go as far as your body will naturally allow you to go. Take a breath when you are bending to the left and then let your breath out to the right. Do not curve and do not contract your back. Only make sure that you bend sideways. You can execute this while standing. Do this exercise for one to two minutes or for a total of twenty-six times. These side bends help stimulate the liver and the colon, all while increasing your spines natural flexibility.

Shoulder Shrugs

In the easy pose, sit on top of your feet and move your shoulders in an up and down movement. Make sure that you are inhaling on up and exhaling on down. Do this for one to two minutes. To end the exercise, inhale on up and hold. Exhale and relax. This is for releasing the tension build-up that dwells inside of your shoulder muscles and in the upper most parts of your back.

Cobra Pose

While lying with your palm's flat underneath your shoulders, take in a breath, and curve your back upward. Point upward with your nose and let your chin follow naturally. Next, bring your body up using your hands to take the weight, feeling each stretch in your spinal column. Keep going until you cannot arch your back anymore. You do not want to strain your back, so only go as far as your body will allow you. It is okay if you have trouble with this at first, as your spine may be stiff. It will loosen up the more you do the exercise. Once you have reached the point where you cannot go any further, breathe in deep and execute the breath of fire. Repeat this for one-hundred and twenty to one-hundred and eighty seconds. Finishing the exercise, take in a breath and hold it. Bring in all your energy up your spine. Blow out the breath and bring your body back down slowly allowing for each part of your back to relax in the process. Rest for the next one to three minutes and allow yourself to feel the benefits of this stretching exercise. This exercise helps strengthen your lower back and removes tension from it.

Spinal Rock and Roll

Sit with your knees as close to your chest as possible and using your arms to hold them close. Begin to lightly rock your body on the floor with your spine. Use this as a means to massage gently from the base of your neck all the way down. Make sure to do this on a soft surface so that you do not injure yourself. Repeat this for one to two minutes. This is an exercise that helps circulate your energy and relax your spine.

Alternating Leg Stretches

Sitting on the floor with your legs wide apart, grab ahold of your toes with your corresponding hands. If you need to grab at the ankles so that you are keeping your legs straight, you can do that alternatively, too. Inhale at the middle and then as you bend to the left blow it out. Inhale again at the middle and while bending to the right blow it out. Make sure the bend is initiated at your hips in order to open up the pelvic region. This also helps avoid simply bending and arching at the spine. Make sure that you are only loosening the muscles and not straining them. Continue doing this with your powerful breathing for sixty to one-hundred and twenty seconds. Finalizing the exercise, breathe in at the middle again and keep the breath longer than normal. Move your energy up your spine and relax. Bring your legs to the center and bounce them then massage them to help further relax the stretched muscles.

The Live Nerve Stretch

With your legs stretched out, draw your right food inward to the inner thigh on your left leg and begin to bring your body down on top of the leg to grab wherever it feels the most comfortable. Do the breath of fire as you are in this position, keeping your leg as straight on the ground as you can. Do this for one to two minutes on each side. To end the exercise, take a deep breath in and using the power blowing out of the breath to make your stretch even more deep and intense. Then bring yourself to the middle point and repeat for the opposite leg, making sure to deepen the stretch while you blow the breath out. The stretches in this exercise is beneficial for stretching your lower back and your leg muscles.

Cat Cow Stretching

Get on all fours, with your hand's shoulder width apart and palms down to the floor. Inhale and bring your back down while bringing up your head at the same time. When beginning to exhale, bring your spine upward and your head downward. Make sure to keep your arms completely straight during each cat and cow. Continue the exercise using deep and rhythmic breathing. As you become more flexible speed up the process of alternating between the cat and the cow. Do this in repetition for one to three minutes.

The Pick Me Up

Lay in a relaxing position with your back flat on the ground under you. Bring your heels to your rear end by flexing at the knees. Feet should remain flat on the ground while you are doing this. Bring your hips up off of the ground by using your ankles as a support by holding on to them. Make sure to arch your spine and lift your navel upward. As you are lifting up from the ground, slowly breath in through your nostrils. Keep the breath held in as long as you can while gently continuing to push as far upward as your body will comfortably allow. Slowly bring yourself back to relax on the ground while exhaling the same breath through your nose. Slowly repeat this upward and downward lifting motion for at least twelve repetitions. Make sure that you are synchronizing your breathing with the motions of your hips. Do not exceed twenty-six lifts. To increase your total lifts, start with twelve, and gradually increase yourself to twenty-six by one to two per day.

On a side note, if you cannot reach your ankles at this point, that is okay. Flexibility is something that has to be worked toward. You can change this exercise to accommodate your flexibility levels easily. Simply lay with your palms resting flat on the ground to help you push up off of the ground with your hips. This is one of those exercises that you should clear with a doctor when you suffer from chronic back problems. Try your hardest to let your breathing do the work with this exercise. Rest on your back for a few minutes afterward to allow your body to get the full relaxing effect. This exercise is good for strengthening the abdominal muscles and helps give you an immediate boost of energy. This exercise also moves the energy levels from your upper to lower spine and back.

Kundalini Awakening

The ideals of the Kundalini Awakening are that each one of us is unique and creative. We hold inside of us the power and capacity to master and accept our circumstances. We can tap into the powers that are inside of us and achieve happiness and deep inner peace. The spiritual path that we embark on with Kundalini is about connecting with our soul essence, our vital energies, and discovering gifts that can successfully help us navigate our lives.

Kundalini is an energy that lays dormant in all of us until we tap into it. This is the energy that ignites our souls and awakens all of our consciousnesses. Learning how to raise your inner Kundalini is about getting your internal flame to ignite and allowing your passion for life to be unleashed. The only way to achieve this is to tame the emotions that run wild on the outside by learning how to discipline ourselves and allow the inner energy to fulfill our life.

Our soul's spirit is always available to us. Kundalini yoga was designed to help us tap into the magical powers of the Divine that live inside of us, keep our internal flame cultivated, make a charismatic presence to build upon, unleash our abilities to create our own way, allow us to act accordingly, use our fears to transfer energy and vitality, and awaken the power of our soul.

The Awakening Process

The Kundalini awakening process consists of three specific steps: activation, allowing, and alignment. Since this boundless amount of energy lies dormant in our souls, it requires these three complementary principles to be awakened.

Activation is the masculine aspect or conscious effort. This is the practicing of techniques that are designed to shift the energy. In order for activation to work, it requires some sort of action or doing to work.

Allowing is the acceptance of what is occurring in the conscious mind. Allowing is also known as the feminine

aspect. Allowing is simply allowing things to happen and being aware of them happening.
Alignment is the result of the activation and the allowing. The goal is to align our personal energy with the universal energy so that this energy flows through us without any effort and to align our minds, bodies, and emotions so that the infinite potential that we possess is unleased.

Activation

Activation takes place during the asanas or the exercises themselves. When done correctly and the energy is flowing properly, then that is facilitating the release of the Kundalini. The exercises and their power are enhanced by the careful and powerful breathing techniques and the reciting of mantras. These exercises serve to help strengthen your nervous system, allow the glands to secrete the necessary hormones, loosen the muscles, all while aligning the body's skeleton. With this in mind, the idea is that the body is the temple of the soul.

Allowing

Allowing is what happens when relaxation occurs, and we let go. This is what happens when we stop trying to make something happen and just allow things to happen as they come. As a general rule, we are programmed to try to control ourselves and our emotions, the events that surround us, and everything in our environment. However, most of what actually happens is beyond our control. By simply letting go and allowing the energy to flow, we are expanding our awareness of what is happening around us and we release our resistance to what prevents our energy from flowing freely. This allows us to have happiness in our lives.

Alignment

Alignment is both an active and passive action. The active part of alignment is applying the locks, which is allowing subtle movements among the chakras that are positioned along the spine. The passive part is what happens naturally to the body when these have been released. The physical and energy bodies are automatically aligned when this happens, and the resistance that held them apart is gone allowing them to flow freely from the Kundalini point through the top of the head.

The Signs of an Awakening

- You find your mind beginning to circle. It is the beginning of an emotional reckoning. The circumstances of your life in the past that give you extreme emotions, like missing something or mourning for something, keep coming back for you to think about.
- You begin to unpack years of built-up energy that prevented you from being present in the past. This means that you are going to spend a lot of time thinking about the past; this is the time for you to come to peace with it and allow it to go.
- You may start to randomly wake in the middle of the night. There may be crying and shots of energy going up your spine. There may even be bouts of intense sweating. These are physically normal changes that occur to your body during an awakening.
- You feel like you need to start making drastic changes in your life. These may seem radical to

some. Intense dieting and even who you associate with can be changes you make. You are making these changes because you are noticing what is not working out in your life anymore.

- You begin to make the realization that your mind has been what has held you and your feelings back for so long. You begin to realize that you have been trapped by your ego and trying to prepare for the worst when it was only just your mind sabotaging you.
- Things in your life begin to just start working out naturally without you having to control everything.
- Your empathic ability seems to become keener. You begin to feel what others around you are feeling and experiencing what they are experiencing. It can be overwhelming to you at first, but this is the sign that your third eye is opening, which is what is connecting you to your true nature.
- You constantly want to be outside. It is an urge that you cannot control.
- You feel like decluttering your life is a top priority. Anything that has caused holding you back, whatever it may be, you feel the need to let it go.

- You begin to start questioning things in your life like politics, religion, and tradition. You may not have known the root of your need for these things, but you will begin to figure out what spot they hold in your life.
- You experience random bouts with emotion. The truth is that you are trying to work through old feelings that were never fully addressed.
- You begin to feel strong, angry emotions for what you were and what you weren't given in life. You feel it for all the pain you caused and didn't cope with. Eventually, once you work through this anger, you will find that it will turn into acceptance. You will recognize that it was all part of the journey.
- You begin realizing that life was never something that was happening to you, but that it was just a reflection of you. What you put into the world is what you are going to get back.
- You feel a connection with the divine. You see yourself as godly and recognize the godliness in every other human being you come into contact with.

- You realize that you cannot wait to actually start living your life. You understand that your life is happening right now and that it always has been. You realize that you have missed out on large amounts of joy because you were waiting for something that had already begun to begin.

What Happens Once You Are Awake?

Once you have reached the full capacity of the Kundalini awakening, you will find that there a lot of changes that occur in your life. These are both physical and mental things that happen. You may not understand them at first, but once you become in tune with them and fully understand what it means, then you can fully embrace them.

- When you have fully awakened your Kundalini, you will begin to feel more at peace, and bliss will come easily to you. It is important to allow yourself to feel those things and when fully awake, you will be able to do it without thinking about it.
- You will have an increased IQ level. It is not because you are smarter, but because the things

that you kept locked down in your mind are finally free to escape.

- You will notice that the things around you seem brighter and louder. This is because once your Kundalini is awakened, you have also awakened the senses that you have hindered with your efforts to control everything. The lights will be lighter, the colors brighter, and the sounds louder.
- You will begin to feel as if you are purer. The things that once made you feel unclean will melt away, and you will feel as if they never existed.
- Your ability for the supernatural will be enhanced. Once you are in tune with your own cosmic power, the universe's cosmic powers will feel natural.
- Your abilities to be more compassionate and more empathetic toward people will be increased. This is because you have shed your own reservations about your own feelings and can be more open to other people's feelings.
- An awakening can help slow down the aging process and increase your level of creativity.
- The sounds that you hear almost on a regular basis will be the gentle and peaceful vibrations that come with having a stronger inner peace.

- You have the increased ability to attract people and situations by simply using your thoughts.
- You find that your spiritual connections seem to be more increased.

Awakening and Others

The awakening that you undergo can affect the people that are around you. Once your energy is activated, it changes the vibrations and the frequencies around you which can invade another person's energy field.

When someone else does not have their Kundalini energies awakened, and their chakras have not been opened, feeling your vibrations may actually come across to them as intense sexual energy. This can happen to anyone at any time when they have not awoken their own chakras.

It is possible for other people to also feel like they have begun an awakening when they have not. Sometimes it is possible that your awakening is still so new and so strong that you are not sure how to harness all of your energy and feelings that it deflects on to those around you. This isn't always the case, but it has happened.

Conclusion

Congratulations on making it to the end of *Astrology for Beginners: The Ultimate Guide to Astrology, Zodiac Signs, Numerology, and Kundalini Rising.* At this point, you have learned all the basics of finding what creates you as a person on the astrological plane.

Astrology holds a lot of answers to the questions of our lives and the paths we are supposed to take. The Zodiac signs that are explained by the astrological information derived from our birthday and the exact moment in time that we were born can tell us a lot about ourselves. There are many interpretations as to astrology and the zodiac across cultures as well.

If you were searching for an even deeper level to yourself, you learned that Numerology is where you will find it. Your birth date, full name, and day of birth can tell you a plethora of things about yourself. All of these work hand in hand to create a chart, but unless you are a skilled numerologist, you should only stick to interpreting the basics.

Kundalini helps you release your energies out to the world. There are certain poses and breathing techniques to follow, but once the discipline has been mastered, you can begin to feel the peace that you were meant to feel. There is a large world out there, and this only skims the surface of that, but the amount of information that has been poured into this book will give you all of the tools you need to help you identify if you are on the right path.

We hope that this journey has given you all of the answers that you are looking for in your life. We also hope that you begin the journey of awakening your own cosmic energy so that you can live your best life!

Printed in Poland
by Amazon Fulfillment
Poland Sp. z o.o., Wrocław

55798469R00103